THE HOLY YEAR
of
MERCY

A
Faith-Sharing Guide

—⚬⚬⚬—

With Reflections
by Pope Francis

THE
HOLY YEAR
of
MERCY

A
Faith-Sharing Guide

*With Reflections
by Pope Francis*

Compiled by Susan Heuver

the WORD
among us®
press

Published by The Word Among Us Press
7115 Guilford Road
Frederick, Maryland 21704
www.wau.org

19 18 17 16 15   4 5 6 7 8

ISBN: 978-1-59325-282-3
eISBN: 978-1-59325-475-9

Nihil obstat: The Reverend Monsignor Michael Morgan
                    Censor Librorum
                    July 13, 2015
Imprimatur: The Most Reverence Felipe J. Estévez, STD
                    Bishop of St. Augustine
                    July 13, 2015

Cover design by Andrea Alvarez
Corbis Images

Made and printed in the United States of America

Library of Congress Control Number: 2015945853

Contents

Introduction / 7

Prayer of Pope Francis for the Jubilee of Mercy / 10

Session 1: God's Mercy Is for Everyone / 12

Session 2: That First Gaze of Mercy / 24

Session 3: Cleansed by God's Mercy / 36

Session 4: Christ's Wounds of Mercy / 50

Session 5: Compassion: The Touch of Mercy / 62

Session 6: Mercy Is Greater than Prejudice / 72

Session 7: The Patience of Mercy / 86

Session 8: Mercy and New Life / 98

Appendix 1: *The Face of Mercy*, Bull of Indiction of the
Extraordinary Jubilee of Mercy / 110

Appendix 2: The Logo and Motto for the Jubilee Year / 140

Appendix 3: Practical Pointers for Faith-Sharing Groups / 142

INTRODUCTION

Pope Francis continually reminds us that Jesus came to seek and save the lost. Like the good shepherd pursuing his wayward sheep and the father running to embrace his prodigal son, God our Father mercifully goes out to find his lost children so that none should perish. God's boundless mercy has become the recurring theme of Pope Francis' preaching and teaching. He so desires that we understand the mercy of God that he has designated December 8, 2015, through November 20, 2016, as an Extraordinary Jubilee of Mercy.

Pope Francis not only speaks of God's mercy at every opportunity, he also manifests it in his own actions. Whether he is washing the feet of prisoners, embracing people with disabilities, or calling suffering Catholics on his cell phone, the Holy Father has demonstrated the deeds that should flow from a heart that is "merciful like the Father"—the motto for the Holy Year.

To help Catholics enter into this Year of Mercy, we have collected eight of Pope Francis' homilies that focus on the theme of experiencing and sharing God's mercy. Some are based on Gospel passages that one would expect, like Jesus' encounter with the woman at the well. Others are more surprising choices, like the parable of the weeds and the wheat or Jesus' cleansing of the Temple. But God's mercy shines through all of them.

In the Bull of Indiction, the formal papal announcement of the Jubilee Year, Pope Francis tells us that Jesus Christ is the face of the Father's mercy. By teaching us to recognize God's mercy in Jesus' many conversations and actions, Pope Francis helps us recognize God's mercy in the varied circumstances of our own lives. In a world that is so filled with turmoil and suffering, we need to experience God's mercy in our everyday lives and bring that mercy to others. Pope Francis reminds us that God never stops or goes halfway in showing mercy to his children, and he calls us to do the same.

How to Use this Faith-Sharing Guide

This book is designed to be a simple, easy-to-use study guide that is also challenging and thought provoking. It can be used individually for personal reflection and study, with a friend, or in a small faith-sharing group. The guide is divided into eight sessions, each focused on a particular insight into God's mercy.

Whether you use this guide alone or in a group, be sure to begin each session with prayer. You may wish to use Pope Francis' prayer found on pages 10–11. Ask God to open his word to you and speak to you personally. Read the Scripture passage slowly and carefully. Then, take as much time as you need to meditate on the passage and pursue any thoughts it brings to mind. When you are ready, move on to the commentary from Pope Francis. Ponder his words and reflect on God's mercy.

Each session contains two sets of questions to help you understand the Scripture passage and discover its relevance to your life. Those questions under the heading "Understand!" focus on the text itself and help you grasp what it means. "Grow!" questions are intended to elicit a personal response by helping you examine your life in light of the truths that you uncover. Under the headings "Reflect!" and "Act!," we offer suggestions to help you respond concretely to the passage.

Pertinent quotations from Pope Francis' Bull of Indiction for the Extraordinary Jubilee of Mercy, entitled *Misericordiae Vultus* [The Face of Mercy], appear in each session. The complete text of the Bull can be found in Appendix 1. This rich and moving document will add new layers of understanding and insight to your study. You may also want to view the logo for the Jubilee Year in Appendix 2 and read an explanation of its meaning.

As is true with any learning resource, you will benefit most by writing your answers to the questions in the spaces provided. This can help you formulate your thoughts more clearly and will give you a record of your reflections and spiritual growth that you can return to in the future to recall how much God has accomplished in your life. End your reading or study with a prayer thanking God for what you have learned, and ask the Holy Spirit to help you live out the call to be a missionary of mercy in the world today.

The format of this guide is especially well suited for use in small groups. Some recommendations and practical tips for Bible study discussion groups are offered in Appendix 3.

We hope that *The Holy Year of Mercy* will open your eyes to the mercy of the Father in the face of Jesus and draw you into deeper prayer and communion with God. Through this faith-sharing guide, may you come to experience God's mercy and share it with those around you.

Susan Heuver
The Word Among Us Press

Prayer of Pope Francis for the Jubilee of Mercy

Lord Jesus Christ,
you have taught us to be merciful like the heavenly Father,
and have told us that whoever sees you sees Him.
Show us your face and we will be saved.
Your loving gaze freed Zacchaeus and Matthew from being
    enslaved by money;
the adulteress and Magdalene from seeking happiness only
    in created things;
made Peter weep after his betrayal,
and assured Paradise to the repentant thief.
Let us hear, as if addressed to each one of us,
    the words that you spoke to the Samaritan woman:
"If you knew the gift of God!"

You are the visible face of the invisible Father,
of the God who manifests his power above all
    by forgiveness and mercy:
let the Church be your visible face in the world,
    its Lord risen and glorified.
You willed that your ministers would also be
    clothed in weakness
in order that they may feel compassion for those
    in ignorance and error:
let everyone who approaches them feel sought after,
    loved, and forgiven by God.

Send your Spirit and consecrate every one of us
    with its anointing,
so that the Jubilee of Mercy may be a year of grace
    from the Lord,
and your Church, with renewed enthusiasm,
may bring good news to the poor,
proclaim liberty to captives and the oppressed,
and restore sight to the blind.

We ask this through the intercession of Mary,
    Mother of Mercy,
you who live and reign with the Father and the Holy Spirit
    for ever and ever.
Amen.

Session 1

GOD'S MERCY IS FOR EVERYONE

MERCIFUL LIKE THE FATHER

"With how much love he heals
our sinful heart!"

—POPE FRANCIS

Luke 7:36-50

36 One of the Pharisees asked him to eat with him, and he went into the Pharisee's house, and sat at table. 37 And behold, a woman of the city, who was a sinner, when she learned that he was sitting at table in the Pharisee's house, brought an alabaster flask of ointment, 38 and standing behind him at his feet, weeping, she began to wet his feet with her tears, and wiped them with the hair of her head, and kissed his feet, and anointed them with the ointment. 39 Now when the Pharisee who had invited him saw it, he said to himself, "If this man were a prophet, he would have known who and what sort of woman this is who is touching him, for she is a sinner." 40 And Jesus answering said to him, "Simon, I have something to say to you." And he answered, "What is it, Teacher?" 41 "A certain creditor had two debtors; one owed five hundred denarii, and the other fifty. 42 When they could not pay, he forgave them both. Now which of them will love him more?" 43 Simon answered, "The one, I suppose, to whom he forgave more." And he said to him, "You have judged rightly." 44 Then turning toward the woman he said to Simon, "Do you see this woman? I entered your house, you gave me no water for my feet, but she has wet my feet with her tears and wiped them with her hair. 45 You gave me no kiss, but from the time I came in she has not ceased to kiss my feet. 46 You did not anoint my head with oil, but she has anointed my feet with ointment. 47 Therefore I tell you, her sins, which are many, are forgiven, for she loved much; but he who is forgiven little, loves little." 48 And he said to her, "Your sins are forgiven." 49 Then those

who were at table with him began to say among themselves, "Who is this, who even forgives sins?" [50] And he said to the woman, "Your faith has saved you; go in peace."

Words of Pope Francis

This year again, . . . we are gathered to celebrate the penitential liturgy. We are united with the many Christians who, today, in every part of the world, have accepted the invitation to live this moment as a sign of the Lord's goodness. The Sacrament of Reconciliation, indeed, allows us to draw near to the Father with trust to have the certainty of his forgiveness. He is truly "rich in mercy" and extends it abundantly upon those who appeal to him with a sincere heart. . . .

The Gospel we have heard (cf. Luke 7:36-50) opens to us a path of hope and comfort. It is good to feel Jesus' compassionate gaze upon us, just as it was felt by the sinful woman in the house of the Pharisee. In this passage two words persistently return: *love* and *judgment*.

There is the love of the sinful woman who humbles herself before the Lord; but before that is *the merciful love of Jesus* for her, which drives her to approach him. Her tears of repentance and joy wash the feet of the Master, and her hair dries them with gratitude; the kisses are an expression of her pure love; and the perfumed ointment poured in abundance attests to how precious he is in her eyes. This woman's every gesture speaks of love and expresses her desire to have unwavering certitude in her life:

that of having been forgiven. And this certitude is beautiful! And Jesus gives her this certitude: in accepting her he demonstrates the love God has for her, just for her, a public sinner! Love and forgiveness are simultaneous: God forgives her many sins, he forgives her for all of them, for "she loved much" (Luke 7:47); and she adores Jesus because she feels that in him there is mercy and not condemnation. She feels that Jesus understands her with love, she who is a sinner. Thanks to Jesus, God lifts her many sins off her shoulders; he no longer remembers them (cf. Isaiah 43:25). For this is also true: when God forgives, he forgets. God's forgiveness is great! For her now a new era begins; through love she is reborn into a new life.

This woman has truly encountered the Lord. In silence, she opened her heart; in sorrow, she showed repentance for her sins; by her tears, she appealed to divine goodness to receive forgiveness. For her there will be no judgment but that which comes from God, and this is the judgment of mercy. The hero of this encounter is certainly love, a mercy which goes beyond justice.

Simon, the master of the house, the Pharisee, on the contrary, *doesn't manage to find the road of love.* Everything is calculated, everything is thought out. . . . He stands firm on the threshold of formality. It is an unpleasant thing, formal love; he doesn't understand. He is not capable of taking that next step forward to meet Jesus who will bring him salvation. Simon limits himself to inviting Jesus to lunch, but did not truly welcome him. In his thoughts Simon invokes only justice, and in doing so, he errs. *His judgment of the woman distances him from the truth* and prevents him from even understanding who his guest is. He stopped at the surface—at formality—incapable of seeing the heart. Before the parable of Jesus and the question of which servant would love more, the Pharisee responds correctly: "The one, I suppose, to whom he forgave more." Jesus doesn't fail to observe: "You have judged rightly" (Luke 7:43). When Simon's judgment is turned to love, then is he in the right.

Jesus' reminder urges each of us never to stop at the surface of things, especially when we have a person before us. We are called to look beyond, *to focus on the heart* in order to see how much generosity everyone is capable of. No one can be excluded from the mercy of God; everyone knows the way to access it, and the Church is the *house where everyone is welcomed and no one is rejected.* Her doors remain wide open, so that those who are touched by grace may find the assurance of forgiveness. The greater the sin, the greater the love that must be shown by the Church to those who repent. With how much love Jesus looks at us! With how much love he heals our sinful heart! Our sins never scare him. Let us consider the prodigal son who, when he decided to return to his father, considers making a speech, but the father doesn't let him speak. He embraces him (cf. Luke 15:17-24). This is the way Jesus is with us. "Father, I have so many sins . . ."—"But he will be glad if you go: he will embrace you with such love! Don't be afraid."

Dear brothers and sisters, I have often thought of how the Church may render more clear her mission to be a witness to mercy; and we have to make this journey. It is a journey which begins with spiritual conversion. Therefore, I have decided to announce an *Extraordinary Jubilee* which has at its center the mercy of God. It will be a *Holy Year of Mercy.* We want to live in the light of the word of the Lord: "Be merciful, even as your Father is merciful" (cf. Luke 6:36). And this especially applies to confessors! So much mercy! . . .

I am confident that the whole Church, which is in such need of mercy, for we are sinners, will be able to find in this Jubilee the joy of rediscovering and rendering fruitful God's mercy, with which we are all called to give comfort to every man and every woman of our time. Do not forget that God *forgives all*, and God *forgives always*. Let us never tire of asking forgiveness. Let us henceforth entrust this Year to the Mother of Mercy, that she turn her gaze upon us and watch over our journey: our penitential journey, our year-long journey with an open heart, to receive the indulgence of God, to receive the mercy of God.

—Homily, St. Peter's Basilica, Celebration of Penance: Communal Reconciliation Service with Individual Confession and Absolution, March 13, 2015

Understand!

1. Why do you think the Pharisee invited Jesus into his home? What do the Pharisee's thoughts about the woman reveal about his interior state and attitude toward Jesus?

2. Why would the sinful woman risk ridicule and rejection in order to anoint Jesus? What could she have heard about Jesus that gave her the courage to approach him? (See the healing of the Roman centurion's slave in Luke 7:1-10 and the healing of a leper in Luke 5:12-16.)

_____

_____

_____

_____

_____

_____

3. Luke provides specific details about the woman's posture and actions as she anoints Jesus' feet. What was Luke trying to show us? What do her actions say about her awareness of her need for mercy and her attitude toward Jesus?

_____

_____

_____

_____

_____

_____

4. Jesus contrasts the woman's actions with those of the Pharisee. What did the woman grasp that the Pharisee failed to understand?

_____

_____

_____
_____
_____
_____

5. What do Jesus' response to the woman and his story about the two debtors teach us about God's heart of mercy?

_____
_____
_____
_____
_____
_____

Grow!

1. Like the Pharisee, have you ever felt curious about Jesus, and yet wanted to keep him at a distance? If so, what made you feel this way?

_____
_____
_____
_____
_____

2. Pope Francis reminds us that God's mercy always precedes our turning to him. It is God's mercy that draws us to him. Have you ever experienced the mercy of God "calling" or "pulling" you to draw closer to our Lord through prayer or the sacraments? If so, when?

_____

_____

_____

_____

_____

_____

3. Pope Francis says that our sins do not scare God, but they can often make us afraid to come close to him. What gives you the courage to trust in God's mercy and return to him?

_____

_____

_____

_____

_____

_____

4. Not everyone has lived a flagrantly immoral life in the way that this woman did, and yet everyone owes an immense debt to Jesus. What causes you to see your need for God's mercy?

_____

_____

_____

_____

_____

_____

5. Do you ever recognize in yourself the Pharisee's attitude of judgment and self-righteousness? How does this keep you from experiencing God's mercy?

_____

_____

_____

_____

_____

Reflect!

1. Read the following passages from the Gospel of Matthew: 5:38-48; 7:1-5; and 8:21-35. How does God's mercy move you to love him more deeply and change the way you treat others?

2. Pope Francis speaks of the ruthless servant in Matthew 18:23-35 who did not show mercy to his fellow servant. He also assures us that God wants us on the path of merciful love because he wants us happy, peaceful, and full of joy. After reflecting on the passage and his words below, ask yourself, "Am I joyful and peaceful? If not, is it because I

have failed to 'let go of anger, wrath, violence, and revenge' and not forgiven someone?"

From another parable, we cull an important teaching for our Christian lives. In reply to Peter's question about how many times it is necessary to forgive, Jesus says: "I do not say seven times, but seventy times seven times" (Matthew 18:22). He then goes on to tell the parable of the "ruthless servant," who, called by his master to return a huge amount, begs him on his knees for mercy. His master cancels his debt. But he then meets a fellow servant who owes him a few cents and who in turn begs on his knees for mercy, but the first servant refuses his request and throws him into jail. When the master hears of the matter, he becomes infuriated and, summoning the first servant back to him, says, "Should not you have had mercy on your fellow servant, as I had mercy on you?" (18:33). Jesus concludes, "So also my heavenly Father will do to every one of you, if you do not forgive your brother from your heart" (18:35).

This parable contains a profound teaching for all of us. Jesus affirms that mercy is not only an action of the Father, it becomes a criterion for ascertaining who his true children are. In short, we are called to show mercy because mercy has first been shown to us. Pardoning offenses becomes the clearest expression of merciful love, and for us Christians it is an imperative from which we cannot excuse ourselves. At times how hard it seems to forgive! And yet pardon is the instrument placed into our fragile hands to attain serenity of heart. To let go of anger, wrath, violence, and revenge are necessary conditions to living joyfully. Let us therefore heed the Apostle's exhortation: "Do not let the sun go down on your anger" (Ephesians 4:26). Above all, let us listen to the words of Jesus who made mercy an ideal of life and a criterion for the credibility of our faith: "Blessed are the merciful, for they shall obtain mercy" (Matthew 5:7): the beatitude to which we should particularly aspire in this Holy Year.

As we can see in Sacred Scripture, mercy is a key word that indicates God's action towards us. He does not limit himself merely to affirming his love, but makes it visible and tangible. Love, after all, can never be just an abstraction. By its very nature, it indicates something concrete: intentions, attitudes, and behaviors that are shown in daily living. The mercy of God is his loving concern for each one of us. He feels responsible; that is, he desires our well-being and he wants to see us happy, full of joy, and peaceful. This is the path which the merciful love of Christians must also travel. As the Father loves, so do his children. Just as he is merciful, so we are called to be merciful to each other. (Bull of Indiction, *The Face of Mercy*, 9)

Act!

Is there a relationship in your life that is poisoned by judgment or bitterness? How is God asking you to see this person differently, with Jesus' eyes of mercy? What steps can you take in order to be merciful as the Father is merciful?

Session 2

THAT FIRST GAZE

OF MERCY

"Returning to Galilee means treasuring
in my heart the living memory of that call,
when Jesus passed my way, gazed at me
with mercy, and asked me to follow him."
—POPE FRANCIS

Matthew 28:1-10

¹Now after the sabbath, toward the dawn of the first day of the week, Mary Magdalene and the other Mary went to see the sepulchre. ²And behold, there was a great earthquake; for an angel of the Lord descended from heaven and came and rolled back the stone, and sat upon it. ³His appearance was like lightning, and his raiment white as snow. ⁴And for fear of him the guards trembled and became like dead men. ⁵But the angel said to the women, "Do not be afraid; for I know that you seek Jesus who was crucified. ⁶He is not here; for he has risen, as he said. Come, see the place where he lay. ⁷Then go quickly and tell his disciples that he has risen from the dead, and behold, he is going before you to Galilee; there you will see him. Lo, I have told you." ⁸So they departed quickly from the tomb with fear and great joy, and ran to tell his disciples. ⁹And behold, Jesus met them and said, "Hail!" And they came up and took hold of his feet and worshiped him. ¹⁰Then Jesus said to them, "Do not be afraid; go and tell my brethren to go to Galilee, and there they will see me."

Words of Pope Francis

The Gospel of the resurrection of Jesus Christ [Matthew 28:1-10] begins with the journey of the women to the tomb at dawn on the day after the Sabbath. They go to the tomb to honor the body of the Lord, but they find it open and empty. A mighty angel says to them: "Do not be afraid!" (28:5) and orders them to go and tell the disciples: "He has been raised from the dead, and indeed he is going ahead of you to Galilee" (verse 7). The women quickly depart and on the way Jesus himself meets them and says: "Do not fear; go and tell my brothers to go to Galilee; there they will see me" (verse 10). "Do not be afraid," "Do not fear": these are words that encourage us to open our hearts to receive the message.

After the death of the Master, the disciples had scattered; their faith had been utterly shaken, everything seemed over, all their certainties had crumbled and their hopes had died. But now that message of the women, incredible as it was, came to them like a ray of light in the darkness. The news spread: Jesus is risen as he said. And then there was his command to go to *Galilee*; the women had heard it twice, first from the angel and then from Jesus himself: "Let them go to Galilee; there they will see me." "Do not fear" and "Go to Galilee."

Galilee is *the place where they were first called, where everything began!* To return there, to return to the place where they were originally called. Jesus had walked along the shores of the lake as the fishermen were casting their nets. He had called them, and they left everything and followed him (cf. Matthew 4:18-22).

To return to Galilee means *to re-read* everything on the basis of the cross and its victory, fearlessly: "Do not be afraid." To re-read everything—Jesus' preaching, his miracles, the new community, the excitement and the defections, even the betrayal—to re-read everything starting from the end, which is a new beginning, *from this supreme act of love.*

For each of us, too, there is a "Galilee" at the origin of our journey with Jesus. "To go to Galilee" means something beautiful; it means rediscovering our baptism as a living fountainhead, drawing new energy from the sources of our faith and our Christian experience. To return to Galilee means above all to return to that blazing light with which God's grace touched me at the start of the journey. From that flame I can light a fire for today and every day, and bring heat and light to my brothers and sisters. That flame ignites a humble joy, a joy which sorrow and distress cannot dismay, a good, gentle joy.

In the life of every Christian, after baptism there is also another "Galilee," *a more existential "Galilee"*: the experience of a *personal encounter with Jesus Christ* who called me to follow him and to share in his mission. In this sense, returning to Galilee means treasuring in my heart the living memory of that call, when Jesus passed my way, gazed at me with mercy, and asked me to follow him. To return there means reviving the memory of that moment when his eyes met mine, the moment when he made me realize that he loved me.

Today, tonight, each of us can ask: *What is my Galilee?* I need to remind myself, to go back and remember. *Where is my Galilee?* Do I remember it? Have I forgotten it? Seek and you will find it! There the Lord is waiting for you. Have I gone off on roads and paths which made me forget it? Lord, help me: tell me what my Galilee is, for you know that I want to return there to encounter you and to let myself be embraced by your mercy. Do not be afraid, do not fear, return to Galilee!

The Gospel is very clear: we need to go back there, to see Jesus risen, and to become witnesses of his resurrection. This is not to go back in time; it is not a kind of nostalgia. It is returning to our first love, in order to *receive the fire* which Jesus has kindled in the world and to bring that fire to all people, to the very ends of the earth. Go back to Galilee, without fear!

"Galilee of the Gentiles" (Matthew 4:15; Isaiah 8:23)! Horizon of the risen Lord, horizon of the Church; intense desire of encounter . . . Let us be on our way!

—Homily, St. Peter's Basilica, Easter Vigil, April 19, 2014

Understand!

1. Women are the first witnesses of the resurrection. Why do you think the women went to the tomb and not the other disciples? How was this a sign of God's mercy?

_____

_____

_____

_____

_____

2. Why did Matthew include an earthquake in his account of Jesus' resurrection? What might it signify (see Matthew 27:51)?

_____

_____

_____

_____

_____

_____

3. The angel addresses the women by first saying, "Do not be afraid" (Matthew 28:5), and then proclaims to them that Jesus is risen. What fears might have prevented the women from receiving the message of the resurrection?

_____

_____

_____

_____

_____

_____

4. Once the women see the empty tomb, they are sent to tell the disciples that Jesus is risen. How do the angel's words and actions give the women the courage to proclaim the good news of the resurrection?

_____

_____

_____

_____

_____

_____

5. Why does Matthew emphasize that Jesus meets the women *on their way*—while obeying the angel's direction?

_____

_____

_____

_____

_____

_____

Grow!

1. Outside of your baptism, where was the "origin" of your journey with Jesus? Can you name a specific time or place, or was it a gradual awakening to the mercy and grace of the Lord?

_____

_____

_____

_____

_____

_____

2. What is the value in going back to your "Galilee," either your first encounter with Jesus and his mercy or at another time on your journey? What is your response to the Lord as you recall and re-live that encounter?

_____

_____

_____

_____

_____

_____

3. Jesus again tells the women, "Do not be afraid," and repeats their commission to witness to his disciples. How do you respond to God's call to witness to others? What fears do you have?

_____

_____

_____

_____

_____

4. The women had known Jesus before this incident. Yet "they worshiped him" (Matthew 28:9) when he appeared to them after the resurrection. How does this response show that their understanding had changed? How has your encounter with Jesus' mercy changed the way you pray or receive the sacraments?

_____

_____

_____

_____

_____

_____

5. The angel in Matthew's Gospel tells the women that Jesus is going ahead of them to Galilee. We often experience anxiety about the future and feel alone. What does it mean to you that Jesus "goes ahead" of you and waits to encounter you in your future circumstances?

_____

_____

_____

_____

_____

_____

Reflect!

1. All four Gospel writers include the women disciples present at Jesus' death, burial, and resurrection. This was unusual in Jesus' culture and time. What does this tell you about their initial encounter and relationship with Jesus? What does this tell you about Jesus himself?

2. The purpose of the Year of Mercy is that we would encounter Christ anew and bring the fire of his mercy to all the world. How can you carve out more time to sit in prayer to encounter the merciful God who loves you? Prayerfully

read the following from Pope Francis' Bull of Indiction and contemplate God's mercy.

Jesus Christ is the face of the Father's mercy. These words might well sum up the mystery of the Christian faith. Mercy has become living and visible in Jesus of Nazareth, reaching its culmination in him. The Father, "rich in mercy" (Ephesian 2:4), after having revealed his name to Moses as "a God merciful and gracious, slow to anger, and abounding in steadfast love and faithfulness" (Exodus 34:6), has never ceased to show, in various ways throughout history, his divine nature. In the "fullness of time" (Galatians 4:4), when everything had been arranged according to his plan of salvation, he sent his only Son into the world, born of the Virgin Mary, to reveal his love for us in a definitive way. Whoever sees Jesus sees the Father (cf. John 14:9). Jesus of Nazareth, by his words, his actions, and his entire person, reveals the mercy of God.

We need constantly to contemplate the mystery of mercy. It is a wellspring of joy, serenity, and peace. Our salvation depends on it. Mercy: the word reveals the very mystery of the Most Holy Trinity. Mercy: the ultimate and supreme act by which God comes to meet us. Mercy: the fundamental law that dwells in the heart of every person who looks sincerely into the eyes of his brothers and sisters on the path of life. Mercy: the bridge that connects God and man, opening our hearts to the hope of being loved forever despite our sinfulness.

At times we are called to gaze even more attentively on mercy so that we may become a more effective sign of the Father's action in our lives. For this reason I have proclaimed an *Extraordinary Jubilee of Mercy* as a special time for the Church, a time when the witness of believers might grow stronger and more effective. (Bull of Indiction, *The Face of Mercy*, 1–3)

Act!

Share with someone the story of your encounter with Jesus, and ask that person to tell you their own.

Session 3

CLEANSED BY GOD'S MERCY

"Jesus cleanses with tenderness, mercy, love. Mercy is his way of cleansing."

—POPE FRANCIS

John 2:13-25

¹³ The Passover of the Jews was at hand, and Jesus went up to Jerusalem. ¹⁴ In the temple he found those who were selling oxen and sheep and pigeons, and the money-changers at their business. ¹⁵ And making a whip of cords, he drove them all, with the sheep and oxen, out of the temple; and he poured out the coins of the money-changers and overturned their tables. ¹⁶ And he told those who sold the pigeons, "Take these things away; you shall not make my Father's house a house of trade." ¹⁷ His disciples remembered that it was written, "Zeal for thy house will consume me." ¹⁸ The Jews then said to him, "What sign have you to show us for doing this?" ¹⁹ Jesus answered them, "Destroy this temple, and in three days I will raise it up." ²⁰ The Jews then said, "It has taken forty-six years to build this temple, and will you raise it up in three days?" ²¹ But he spoke of the temple of his body. ²² When therefore he was raised from the dead, his disciples remembered that he had said this; and they believed the scripture and the word which Jesus had spoken.

²³ Now when he was in Jerusalem at the Passover feast, many believed in his name when they saw the signs which he did; ²⁴ but Jesus did not trust himself to them, ²⁵ because he knew all men and needed no one to bear witness of man; for he himself knew what was in man.

Words of Pope Francis

Today's Gospel presents the episode of the expulsion of the merchants from the Temple (John 2:13-25). Jesus made "a whip of cords, he drove them all, with the sheep and oxen, out of the temple" (verse 15), the money, everything. Such a gesture gave rise to strong impressions in the people and in the disciples. It clearly appeared as a *prophetic gesture,* so much so that some of those present asked Jesus: "What sign have you to show us for doing this?" (verse 18), who are you to do these things? Show us a sign that you have authority to do them. They were seeking a divine and prodigious sign that would confirm that Jesus was sent by God. And he responded: "Destroy this temple, and in three days I will raise it up" (verse 19). They replied: "It has taken forty-six years to build this temple, and you will raise it up in three days?" (verse 20). They did not understand that the Lord was referring to the *living temple of his body,* that would be destroyed in the death on the cross, but would be raised on the third day. Thus, in three days. "When therefore he was raised from the dead, his disciples remembered that he had said this; and they believed the Scripture and the word Jesus had spoken" (verse 22).

In effect, this gesture of Jesus and his prophetic message are fully understood in the light of his paschal mystery. We have here, according to the evangelist John, the first proclamation of the death and resurrection of Christ: his body, destroyed on the cross by the violence of sin, *will become in the resurrection the universal meeting place between God and mankind.* And the risen Christ is himself the universal meeting place—for everyone!—between God and mankind. For this reason, his humanity is the true temple where God is revealed, speaks, is encountered; and the true worshippers, the *true worshippers* of God are not only the guardians of the material Temple, the keepers of power and of religious knowledge, [but] they are *those who worship God "in spirit and truth"* (John 4:23). . . .

Let us walk in the world as Jesus did, and let us make our whole existence a sign of our love for our brothers, especially the weakest and poorest; *let us build for God a temple of our lives.* And so we make it "encounterable" for those who we find along our journey. If we are witnesses of the living Christ, so many people will encounter Jesus in us, in our witness.

But, we ask—and each one of us can ask ourselves—does the Lord feel at home in my life? Do we allow him to "cleanse" our hearts and to drive out the idols, those attitudes of cupidity, jealousy, worldliness, envy, hatred, those habits of gossiping and tearing down others? Do I allow him to cleanse all the behaviors that are against God, against our neighbor, and against ourselves, as we heard today in the first reading? [Exodus 20:1-17] Each one can answer for him/herself, in the silence of his/her heart: "Do I allow Jesus to make my heart a little cleaner?" "Oh Father, I fear the rod!" But Jesus never strikes. Jesus cleanses with tenderness, mercy, love. Mercy is his way of cleansing. Let us, each of us, let us allow the Lord to enter with his mercy—not with the whip, no, with his mercy—to cleanse our hearts. With us, Jesus' whip is his mercy. Let us open to him the gates so that he will make us a little purer.

Every Eucharist that we celebrate with faith makes us grow as a living temple of the Lord, thanks to the communion with his crucified and risen Body. Jesus recognizes what is in each of us, and knows well our most ardent desires: that of being inhabited by him, only by him. Let us allow him to enter into our lives, into our families, into our hearts. May Mary most holy, the privileged dwelling place of the Son of God, accompany us and sustain us on the Lenten journey, so that we might be able to rediscover the beauty of the encounter with Christ, the only One who frees us and saves us.

—Angelus Address, St. Peter's Square,
Third Sunday of Lent, March 8, 2015

In the Gospel passage that we heard [John 2:13-25], there are two things that strike me: an image and a word. The image is that of Jesus, with whip in hand, driving out all those who took advantage of the Temple to do business. These profiteers who sold animals for sacrifices, changed coins . . . There was the sacred—the Temple, sacred—and this filth, outside. This is the image. And Jesus takes the whip and goes forth, to somewhat cleanse the Temple.

And the phrase, the word, is there where it says that so many people believe in him, a horrible phrase: "but Jesus did not trust himself to them, because he knew all men and needed no one to bear witness of man; for he himself knew what was in man" (John 2:24-25).

We cannot deceive Jesus. He knows us from within. He did not trust them. He, Jesus, did not trust them. And this can be a fine mid-Lenten question: Can Jesus trust himself to me? Can Jesus trust me, or am I two-faced? Do I play the Catholic, one close to the Church, and then live as a pagan? "But Jesus doesn't know; no one goes and tells him about it." He knows. "He needed no one to bear witness; indeed, he knew what was in man." Jesus knows all that there is in our heart. We cannot deceive Jesus. In front of him, we cannot pretend to be saints, and close our eyes, act like this, and then live a life that is not what he wants. And he knows. And we all know the name he gave to those who had two faces: hypocrites.

It will do us good today to enter our hearts and look at Jesus. To say to him: "Lord, look, there are good things, but there are also things that aren't good. Jesus, do you trust me? I am a sinner . . . " This doesn't scare Jesus. If you tell him: "I'm a sinner," it doesn't scare him. What distances him is one who is two-faced: showing him/herself as just in order to cover up hidden sin. "But I go to church, every Sunday, and I . . . " Yes, we can say all of this. But if your heart isn't just, if you don't do justice, if you don't love those who need love, if you do not live according to the spirit of the Beatitudes, you are not Catholic. You are a hypocrite. First: can Jesus trust himself to me? In prayer, let us ask him: Lord, do you trust me?

Second, the gesture. When we enter our hearts, we find things that aren't okay, things that aren't good, as Jesus found that filth of profiteering, of the profiteers, in the Temple. Inside of us too, there are unclean things, there are sins of selfishness, of arrogance, pride, greed, envy, jealousy . . . so many sins! We can even continue the dialogue with Jesus: "Jesus, do you trust me? I want you to trust me. Thus I open the door to you, and you cleanse my soul." Ask the Lord that, as he went to cleanse the Temple, he may come to cleanse your soul. We imagine that he comes with a whip of cords. . . . No, he doesn't cleanse the soul with that! Do you know what kind of whip Jesus uses to cleanse our soul? Mercy. Open your heart to Jesus' mercy! Say: "Jesus, look how much filth! Come, cleanse. Cleanse with your mercy, with your tender words, cleanse with your caresses." If we open our heart to Jesus' mercy, in order to cleanse our heart, our soul, Jesus will trust himself to us.

—Homily, Pastoral Visit to the Roman Parish
Santa Maria Madre del Redentore a Tor Bella Monaca,
Third Sunday of Lent, March 8, 2015

Understand!

1. Why would Jesus have been so angry with those in the Temple courts selling animals for sacrifice and exchanging money to pay the Temple tax? Didn't the Law of Moses require these offerings?

_____

_____

_____

_____

_____

_____

2. John 2:25 tells us that Jesus knew what was in men's hearts. What do you think Jesus saw in the hearts of those in the

Temple that displeased him? What does Jesus want the people to understand about the proper attitude toward God?

_____

_____

_____

_____

_____

_____

3. Read Psalm 69:9, Psalm 27:4, and Psalm 84:1-4, 10 . What do these verses teach us about how the psalmist and Jesus himself viewed the dwelling place of God? In light of this, what can you interpret from Jesus' zeal in cleansing the Temple?

_____

_____

_____

_____

_____

_____

4. Through the prophet Jeremiah, God enumerates the sins of the people, and then he says, "Will you . . . come and stand before me in this house, which is called by my name, and say, 'We are delivered!'—only to go on doing all these abominations? Has this house, which is called by my name, become a den of robbers in your eyes?" (Jeremiah 7:9-11). Jesus refers to this passage when he cleanses the temple.

What does this indicate about the connection between our worship of God and our behavior toward our neighbor?

_____

_____

_____

_____

_____

_____

5. The cleansing of the Temple is an unusual selection to choose as an illustration of God's mercy. In Luke 13:33-34 and 19:41-44, Jesus weeps over Jerusalem, grieving because they have failed to recognize God in their midst. How does this help us understand Jesus' cleansing of the Temple as an expression of his mercy?

_____

_____

_____

_____

_____

_____

Grow!

1. What is the state of your "temple"? Does the Lord feel "at home" in you? Are there areas in your life that you wouldn't want Jesus to enter?

_____

_____

_____

_____

_____

_____

2. Pope Francis bluntly tells us that nothing is hidden from God. Yet God offers us mercy if we would only return to him. God's cleansing, he says, comes not "with the whip of cords," but with his mercy. Is this the way you commonly think about God reacting when you admit and repent of your sins?

_____

_____

_____

_____

_____

_____

3. If you are a temple of God, others should be able to see and encounter the presence of Christ in you. Are you "encounterable," as Pope Francis has phrased it? How might you become more transparent and more open to the needs of others so that people see in you a reflection of Christ and his mercy?

_____

_____

_____

_____

_____

_____

4. Pope Francis says that admitting that we are sinners doesn't distance us from God. Do you believe that? Why or why not?

_____

_____

_____

_____

_____

_____

5. In what areas of your life might you be "two-faced"? How might this be hurting your relationship with Jesus? Can Jesus trust himself to you?

_____

_____

_____

_____

_____

_____

Reflect!

1. What has formed your thinking about God that might make you perceive him as a harsh judge? Read Isaiah 1:18, Wisdom 11:23-26, and Psalm 103:8-18. Pray to receive a greater understanding of God's merciful nature.

2. Pope Francis speaks of the joy of finding that which was lost. While you read his words below, consider the picture that Pope Francis draws of the Father. Is this your picture of your heavenly Father? Why do you think God our Father feels such joy when we experience his mercy?

> In the parables devoted to mercy, Jesus reveals the nature of God as that of a Father who never gives up until he has forgiven the wrong and overcome rejection with compassion and mercy. We know these parables well, three in particular: the lost sheep, the lost coin, and the father with two sons (cf.

Luke 15:1-32). In these parables, God is always presented as full of joy, especially when he pardons. In them we find the core of the Gospel and of our faith, because mercy is presented as a force that overcomes everything, filling the heart with love and bringing consolation through pardon. (Bull of Indiction, *The Face of Mercy*, 9)

Act!

When was the last time you received the Sacrament of Reconciliation? Is Jesus' mercy drawing you to confess your sins and be cleansed? Consider going to Confession this week, trusting in Jesus' mercy.

Session 4

CHRIST'S WOUNDS
OF MERCY

"He invites us to enter into the
mystery of these wounds, which is
the mystery of his merciful love."

—POPE FRANCIS

John 20:19-31

[19] On the evening of that day, the first day of the week, the doors being shut where the disciples were, for fear of the Jews, Jesus came and stood among them and said to them, "Peace be with you." [20] When he had said this, he showed them his hands and his side. Then the disciples were glad when they saw the Lord. [21] Jesus said to them again, "Peace be with you. As the Father has sent me, even so I send you." [22] And when he had said this, he breathed on them, and said to them, "Receive the Holy Spirit. [23] If you forgive the sins of any, they are forgiven; if you retain the sins of any, they are retained." [24] Now Thomas, one of the twelve, called the Twin, was not with them when Jesus came. [25] So the other disciples told him, "We have seen the Lord." But he said to them, "Unless I see in his hands the print of the nails, and place my finger in the mark of the nails, and place my hand in his side, I will not believe."

[26] Eight days later, his disciples were again in the house, and Thomas was with them. The doors were shut, but Jesus came and stood among them, and said, "Peace be with you." [27] Then he said to Thomas, "Put your finger here, and see my hands; and put out your hand, and place it in my side; do not be faithless, but believing." [28] Thomas answered him, "My Lord and my God!" [29] Jesus said to him, "Have you believed because you have seen me? Blessed are those who have not seen and yet believe."

[30] Now Jesus did many other signs in the presence of the disciples, which are not written in this book; [31] but these are written

that you may believe that Jesus is the Christ, the Son of God, and that believing you may have life in his name.

Words of Pope Francis

S t. John, who was in the Upper Room with the other disciples on the evening of the first day after the Sabbath, tells us that Jesus came and stood among them, and said, "Peace be with you!" and he showed them his hands and his side (John 20:19-20); he showed them his wounds. And in this way they realized that it was not an apparition: it was truly him, the Lord, and they were filled with joy.

On the eighth day Jesus came once again into the Upper Room and showed his wounds to Thomas, so that he could touch them as he had wished to, in order to believe and thus become himself a witness to the resurrection.

To us also, on this Sunday which St. John Paul II wished to dedicate to Divine Mercy, the Lord shows us, through the Gospel, his wounds. They are *wounds of mercy*. It is true: the wounds of Jesus are wounds of mercy. "With his stripes we are healed" (Isaiah 53:5).

Jesus invites us to behold these wounds, to touch them as Thomas did, to heal our lack of belief. Above all, he invites us to enter into the mystery of these wounds, which is the mystery of his merciful love.

Through these wounds, as in a light-filled opening, we can see the entire mystery of Christ and of God: his passion, his earthly life—filled with compassion for the weak and the sick—his incarnation in the womb of Mary. And we can retrace the whole history of salvation: the prophecies—especially about the Servant of the Lord, the Psalms, the Law and the Covenant; to the liberation from Egypt, to the first Passover and to the blood of the slaughtered lambs; and again from the patriarchs to Abraham, and then all the way back to Abel, whose blood cried out from the earth. All of this we can see in the wounds of Jesus, crucified and risen; with Mary, in her *Magnificat*, we can perceive that "his mercy extends from generation to generation" (cf. Luke 1:50).

Faced with the tragic events of human history, we can feel crushed at times, asking ourselves, "Why?" Humanity's evil can appear in the world like an abyss, a great void: empty of love, empty of goodness, empty of life. And so we ask: how can we fill this abyss? For us it is impossible; only God can fill this emptiness that evil brings to our hearts and to human history. It is Jesus, God made man, who died on the cross and who fills the abyss of sin with the depth of his mercy.

St. Bernard, in one of his commentaries on the Canticle of Canticles (Sermon 61, 3–5: *Opera Omnia*, 2, 150–151), reflects precisely on the mystery of the Lord's wounds, using forceful and even bold expressions which we do well to repeat today. He says that "through these sacred wounds we can see the secret of [Christ's] heart, the great mystery of love, the sincerity of his mercy with which he visited us from on high."

Brothers and sisters, behold the way which God has opened for us to finally go out from our slavery to sin and death, and thus enter into the land of life and peace. Jesus, crucified and risen, is the way, and his wounds are especially full of mercy.

The saints teach us that the world is changed beginning with the conversion of one's own heart, and that this happens through the mercy of God. And so, whether faced with my own sins or the great tragedies of the world, "my conscience would be distressed, but it would not be in turmoil, for I would recall the wounds of the Lord: 'he was wounded for our iniquities' (Isaiah 53:5). What sin is there so deadly that it cannot be pardoned by the death of Christ?" [St. Bernard].

Keeping our gaze on the wounds of the risen Jesus, we can sing with the Church: "His love endures forever" (Psalm 117:2); eternal is his mercy. And with these words impressed on our hearts, let us go forth along the paths of history, led by the hand of our Lord and Savior, our life and our hope.

—Homily, St. Peter's Basilica, Second Sunday of Easter
(Divine Mercy Sunday), April 12, 2015

Understand!

1. The disciples gathered fearfully behind closed doors. Upon appearing to them, Jesus said, "Peace be with you," and then immediately showed the disciples his wounded hands and side. Why would showing them his wounds calm their fears and bring them peace?

_____

_____

_____

_____

_____

2. Jesus reassures his disciples that despite their denials and their fear, they are still his chosen messengers to the world. Then he gives them the Holy Spirit and commissions them. How does this express God's mercy?

_____

_____

_____

_____

_____

_____

3. Jesus is quite persistent in seeking out Thomas and showing him that he is indeed alive. Why do you think Jesus made it a point to reveal his wounds to Thomas?

_____

_____

_____

_____

_____

_____

4. Have you ever thought of Jesus' wounds as "light-filled openings," as Pope Francis calls them—a way to view the whole of salvation history? What new perspective can this bring to your understanding of what God did for you through the death and resurrection of Jesus?

_____

_____

_____

_____

_____

_____

5. Thomas' profession of faith follows directly after he probes Jesus' wounds. How does Jesus' resurrection change everything for Thomas? For the other disciples? For you?

_____

_____

_____

_____

_____

_____

Grow!

1. Thomas didn't believe that Jesus was truly risen from the dead until he touched Jesus' wounds. Are there areas of unbelief in your life that need healing? If so, ask Jesus for healing. How might God's mercy in the Sacrament of Reconciliation help you in this regard?

_____

_____

_____

_____

_____

_____

2. When do you feel a lack of peace in your life? How is the peace that Jesus speaks of related to his mercy? Share a time in your life when you experienced such peace.

_____

_____

_____

_____

_____

3. How do you experience God's mercy filling what Pope Francis calls the "abyss" in your life, those areas "empty of love, empty of goodness, empty of life"? Where do you see such emptiness in the world, and how can you extend your mercy to those places?

_____

_____

_____

_____

_____

4. Just as Jesus pursued Thomas, do you ever sense Jesus pursuing you with his mercy? How might you grow in awareness that God wants to extend his mercy to you at every moment of your life?

_____

_____

_____

_____

_____

5. The disciples feared that they, too, would be arrested because of their relationship with Jesus. In some parts of the world, many Christians today are persecuted simply because they believe in Jesus. Most of us don't face outright persecution, but we can still fear being identified as believers or sharing our faith. In what situations do you

experience a fear of persecution? What could you do to overcome such fears?

_____

_____

_____

_____

_____

_____

Reflect!

1. Pope Francis calls the wounds of Jesus "wounds of mercy," which Jesus freely bore to save us. Read Isaiah 53, which describes the Suffering Servant, by whose wounds we are healed. Then look at a crucifix while you reflect on this Scripture passage, and see the suffering that Jesus endured for love of you.

2. Mary stood at the foot of the cross beholding Jesus' wounds and hearing him speak words of mercy and forgiveness. Mary, the Mother of Mercy, reminds us that God's mercy extends to every generation, "to everyone without exception." Are there people for whom you've been praying that need to know that God's mercy is for them? Read Pope Francis' words below, and pray that through Mary's intercession your family members or friends would know the mercy of God.

My thoughts now turn to the Mother of Mercy. May the sweetness of her countenance watch over us in this Holy Year, so that all of us may rediscover the joy of God's tenderness. No one has penetrated the profound mystery of the incarnation like Mary. Her entire life was patterned after the presence of mercy made flesh. The Mother of the Crucified and Risen One has entered the sanctuary of divine mercy because she participated intimately in the mystery of His love.

Chosen to be the Mother of the Son of God, Mary, from the outset, was prepared by the love of God to be the *Ark of the Covenant* between God and man. She treasured divine mercy in her heart in perfect harmony with her Son Jesus. Her hymn of praise, sung at the threshold of the home of Elizabeth, was dedicated to the mercy of God which extends from "generation to generation" (Luke 1:50). We too were included in those prophetic words of the Virgin Mary. This will be a source of comfort and strength to us as we cross the threshold of the Holy Year to experience the fruits of divine mercy.

At the foot of the cross, Mary, together with John, the disciple of love, witnessed the words of forgiveness spoken by Jesus. This supreme expression of mercy towards those who crucified him shows us the point to which the mercy of God can reach. Mary attests that the mercy of the Son of God knows no bounds and extends to everyone, without exception. (Bull of Indiction, *The Face of Mercy*, 24)

Act!

Like Thomas, Peter needed to come to a deeper faith in God's mercy after denying Jesus three times. In 1 Peter 2:24, Peter speaks of Jesus' wounds: "He himself bore our sins in his body on the tree, that we might die to sin and live to righteousness. By his wounds you have been healed." Peter and Thomas both went on to tell the world of God's mercy. This week choose one of the people for whom you are interceding. Share with them, whether in person, on the phone, or in an e-mail message, how God's mercy has made a difference in your own life. It could be something small or something life changing.

Session 5

COMPASSION:
THE TOUCH OF MERCY

"God's mercy overcomes every barrier and
Jesus' hand touches the leper. He does
not stand at a safe distance and does
not act by delegating, but places himself
in direct contact with our contagion."

—POPE FRANCIS

Mark 1:40-45

⁴⁰ And a leper came to him beseeching him, and kneeling said to him, "If you will, you can make me clean." ⁴¹ Moved with pity, he stretched out his hand and touched him, and said to him, "I will; be clean." ⁴² And immediately the leprosy left him, and he was made clean. ⁴³ And he sternly charged him, and sent him away at once, ⁴⁴ and said to him, "See that you say nothing to any one; but go, show yourself to the priest, and offer for your cleansing what Moses commanded, for a proof to the people." ⁴⁵ But he went out and began to talk freely about it, and to spread the news, so that Jesus could no longer openly enter a town, but was out in the country; and people came to him from every quarter.

Words of Pope Francis

In these Sundays, Mark the Evangelist speaks to us about Jesus' actions against every type of evil, for the benefit of those suffering in body and spirit: the possessed, the sick, sinners. . . . Jesus presents himself as the One who fights and conquers evil wherever he encounters it. In today's Gospel (cf. Mark 1:40-45), this struggle of his confronts an emblematic case, because the sick man is a leper. Leprosy is a contagious and pitiless disease, which disfigures the person, and it was a symbol of impurity: a leper had to stay outside of inhabited centers and make his presence known to passersby. He was marginalized by the civil and religious community. He was like a dead man walking.

The episode of the healing of the leper takes place in three brief phases: the sick man's supplication, Jesus' response, and the result of the miraculous healing. The leper beseeches Jesus, "kneeling," and says to him: "If you will, you can make me clean" (Mark 1:40). Jesus responds to this humble and trusting prayer because his soul is moved to deep pity: *compassion*. "Compassion" is a most profound word: compassion means "to suffer with another." Jesus' heart manifests God's paternal compassion for that man, moving close to him and *touching him*. And this detail is very important. Jesus "stretched out his hand and *touched him*. . . . And immediately the leprosy left him, and he was made clean" (verses 41-42). God's mercy overcomes every barrier and Jesus' hand touches the leper. He does not stand at a safe distance and does not act by delegating, but places himself in direct contact with our contagion, and in precisely this way our ills become the motive for contact: he, Jesus, takes from us our diseased humanity and we take from him his sound and healing humanity. This happens each time we receive a sacrament with faith: the Lord Jesus "touches" us and grants us his grace. In this case we think especially of the Sacrament of Reconciliation, which heals us from the leprosy of sin.

Once again the Gospel shows us what God does in the face of our ills: God does not come to "give a lesson" on pain; neither does he come to eliminate suffering and death from the world; but rather he comes to take upon himself the burden of our human condition and carries it to the end, to free us in a radical and definitive way. This is how Christ fights the world's maladies and suffering: by taking them upon himself and conquering them with the power of God's mercy.

The Gospel of the healing of the leper tells us today that, if we want to be true disciples of Jesus, we are called to become united to him, instruments of his merciful love, overcoming every kind of marginalization. In order to be "imitators of Christ" (cf. 1 Corinthians 11:1) in the face of a poor or sick person, we must not be afraid to look him in the eye and to draw near with tenderness and compassion, and to touch him and embrace him. I have often asked this of people who help others, to do so looking them in the eye, not to be afraid to touch them; that this gesture of help may also be a gesture of communication: we too need to be welcomed by them. A gesture of tenderness, a gesture of compassion . . . Let us ask you: when you help others, do you look them in the eye? Do you embrace them without being afraid to touch them? Do you embrace them with tenderness? Think about this: how do you help? From a distance or with tenderness, with closeness? If evil is contagious, so is goodness. Therefore, there needs to be ever more abundant goodness in us. Let us be infected by goodness and let us spread goodness!

—Angelus Address, St. Peter's Square,
February 15, 2015

Understand!

1. In Jesus' time, lepers were outcasts, excluded from Jewish society. Why would the leper have risked rejection to approach Jesus?

_____

_____

_____

_____

_____

_____

2. Jesus was "moved with pity" (Mark 1:41) and, touching the man with leprosy, healed him. The word "pity" can mean that we feel sorry for someone. How do you think the word is meant in this context?

_____

_____

_____

_____

_____

_____

3. Mark describes Jesus' actions as stretching out his hand to touch the man. What is Mark telling us by including this detail?

_____

_____

_____

_____

_____

_____

4. Jesus did not merely heal the leper; he declared him to be clean. What would that have meant to the leper? What does being declared "clean" mean to you?

_____

_____

_____

_____

_____

5. Jesus instructed the healed man to go to the priest for ritual purification according to the Law of Moses but not to tell him that Jesus had healed him. Why do you think this was the case?

_____

_____

_____

_____

_____

Grow!

1. Have you ever felt like an outcast from God's family? If so, how were you able to experience being restored to fellowship with Christ and his Church?

_____

_____

_____

_____

_____

2. When have you experienced Jesus drawing near to you in your "contagion" and suffering? How did Jesus' touch of mercy change you?

_____

_____

_____

_____

_____

3. The leper was humble yet fully confident that Jesus could heal him. Do you have the courage to approach Jesus and ask for healing? Share a need that you have with a trusted brother or sister in Christ and ask that person to pray with you for God's healing in that area.

_____

_____

_____

_____

_____

4. Pope Francis speaks of Jesus taking on our sufferings, overcoming them and freeing us with his merciful love. How does this challenge the way that you usually view and respond to suffering?

_____

_____

_____

_____

5. Are you ever hesitant or afraid to approach someone who is poor or sick? How is God asking you to leave this way of thinking behind and tenderly reach out to those in need? What gesture of tenderness or compassion could you show to a person in need?

_____

_____

_____

_____

_____

Reflect!

1. Just as they ostracized lepers, people in Jesus' time shunned tax collectors, who collaborated with the Romans and extorted money from their fellow Jews. Yet Jesus called two such tax collectors to follow him: Levi (Matthew), who became one of the twelve apostles, and Zacchaeus, who climbed a tree to see Jesus and later gave half of his possessions to the poor. Read Mark 2:13-17 and Luke 19:1-10. What is Jesus trying to teach the Pharisees about his mission? What is he trying to teach us?

2. How difficult is it for you to look upon others with mercy and compassion? Read Pope Francis' words below about how Jesus showed mercy to the crowds who followed him. What can you do to grow in knowing and responding to the deepest needs of others?

> Jesus, seeing the crowds of people who followed him, realized that they were tired and exhausted, lost and without a guide, and he felt deep compassion for them (cf. Matthew 9:36). On the basis of this compassionate love he healed the sick who were presented to him (cf. 14:14), and with just a few loaves of bread and fish he satisfied the enormous crowd (cf. 15:37). What moved Jesus in all of these situations was nothing other than mercy, with which he read the hearts of those he encountered and responded to their deepest need. When he came upon the widow of Nain taking her son out for burial, he felt great compassion for the immense suffering

of this grieving mother, and he gave back her son by raising him from the dead (cf. Luke 7:15). After freeing the demoniac in the country of the Gerasenes, Jesus entrusted him with this mission: "Go home to your friends, and tell them how much the Lord has done for you, and how he has had mercy on you" (Mark 5:19). The calling of Matthew is also presented within the context of mercy. Passing by the tax collector's booth, Jesus looked intently at Matthew. It was a look full of mercy that forgave the sins of that man, a sinner and a tax collector, whom Jesus chose—against the hesitation of the disciples—to become one of the Twelve. St. Bede the Venerable, commenting on this Gospel passage, wrote that Jesus looked upon Matthew with merciful love and chose him: *miserando atque eligendo*. This expression impressed me so much that I chose it for my episcopal motto. (Bull of Indiction, *The Face of Mercy*, 8)

Act!

At times people in our churches can feel like outcasts, isolated from God's people. Is there someone you know in your parish who needs to experience God's welcoming embrace? How can you, like Jesus, overcome those barriers and be an instrument of mercy?

Session 6
MERCY IS GREATER THAN PREJUDICE

"We must learn this well! Mercy
is greater than prejudice, and
Jesus is so very merciful!"

—POPE FRANCIS

John 4:5-42

[5] So he came to a city of Samaria, called Sychar, near the field that Jacob gave to his son Joseph. [6] Jacob's well was there, and so Jesus, wearied as he was with his journey, sat down beside the well. It was about the sixth hour.

[7] There came a woman of Samaria to draw water. Jesus said to her, "Give me a drink." [8] For his disciples had gone away into the city to buy food. [9] The Samaritan woman said to him, "How is it that you, a Jew, ask a drink of me, a woman of Samaria?" For Jews have no dealings with Samaritans. [10] Jesus answered her, "If you knew the gift of God, and who it is that is saying to you, 'Give me a drink,' you would have asked him, and he would have given you living water." [11] The woman said to him, "Sir, you have nothing to draw with, and the well is deep; where do you get that living water? [12] Are you greater than our father Jacob, who gave us the well, and drank from it himself, and his sons, and his cattle?" [13] Jesus said to her, "Every one who drinks of this water will thirst again, [14] but whoever drinks of the water that I shall give him will never thirst; the water that I shall give him will become in him a spring of water welling up to eternal life." [15] The woman said to him, "Sir, give me this water, that I may not thirst, nor come here to draw."

[16] Jesus said to her, "Go, call your husband, and come here." [17] The woman answered him, "I have no husband." Jesus said to her, "You are right in saying, 'I have no husband'; [18] for you have had five husbands, and he whom you now have is not your husband; this you said truly." [19] The woman said to him, "Sir,

I perceive that you are a prophet. [20] Our fathers worshiped on this mountain; and you say that in Jerusalem is the place where men ought to worship." [21] Jesus said to her, "Woman, believe me, the hour is coming when neither on this mountain nor in Jerusalem will you worship the Father. [22] You worship what you do not know; we worship what we know, for salvation is from the Jews. [23] But the hour is coming, and now is, when the true worshipers will worship the Father in spirit and truth, for such the Father seeks to worship him. [24] God is spirit, and those who worship him must worship in spirit and truth." [25] The woman said to him, "I know that Messiah is coming (he who is called Christ); when he comes, he will show us all things." [26] Jesus said to her, "I who speak to you am he."

[27] Just then his disciples came. They marveled that he was talking with a woman, but none said, "What do you wish?" or "Why are you talking with her?" [28] So the woman left her water jar, and went away into the city, and said to the people, [29] "Come, see a man who told me all that I ever did. Can this be the Christ?" [30] They went out of the city and were coming to him.

[31] Meanwhile the disciples besought him, saying, "Rabbi, eat." [32] But he said to them, "I have food to eat of which you do not know." [33] So the disciples said to one another, "Has any one brought him food?" [34] Jesus said to them, "My food is to do the will of him who sent me, and to accomplish his work. [35] Do you not say, 'There are yet four months, then comes the harvest'? I tell you, lift up your eyes, and see how the fields are already white for harvest. [36] He who reaps receives wages, and gathers fruit for eternal life, so that sower and reaper may rejoice together. [37] For here the saying holds true, 'One sows and another

reaps.' [38] I sent you to reap that for which you did not labor; others have labored, and you have entered into their labor."

[39] Many Samaritans from that city believed in him because of the woman's testimony, "He told me all that I ever did." [40] So when the Samaritans came to him, they asked him to stay with them; and he stayed there two days. [41] And many more believed because of his word. [42] They said to the woman, "It is no longer because of your words that we believe, for we have heard for ourselves, and we know that this is indeed the Savior of the world."

Words of Pope Francis

Today's Gospel [John 4:5-42] presents Jesus' encounter with the Samaritan woman in Sychar, near an old well where the woman went to draw water daily. That day she found Jesus seated, "wearied as he was with his journey" (4:6). He immediately says to her: "Give me a drink" (verse 7). In this way he overcomes the barriers of hostility that existed between Jews and Samaritans and breaks the mold of prejudice against women. This simple request from Jesus is the start of a frank dialogue, through which he enters with great delicacy into the interior world of a person to whom, according to social norms, he should not have spoken. But Jesus does! Jesus is not afraid. When Jesus sees a person, he goes ahead, because he loves. He loves us all. He never hesitates before a person out of prejudice. Jesus sets her own situation before her, not by judging her but by making her feel worthy, acknowledged, and thus arousing in her the desire to go beyond the daily routine.

Jesus' thirst was not so much for water but for the encounter with a parched soul. Jesus needed to encounter the Samaritan woman in order to open her heart: he asks for a drink so as to bring to light her own thirst. The woman is moved by this encounter: she asks Jesus several profound questions that we all carry within but often ignore. We, too, have many questions to ask, but we don't have the courage to ask Jesus! Lent, dear brothers and sisters, is the opportune time to look within ourselves, to understand our truest spiritual needs, and to ask the Lord's help in prayer. The example of the Samaritan woman invites us to exclaim: "Jesus, give me a drink that will quench my thirst forever."

The Gospel says that the disciples marveled that their Master was speaking to this woman. But the Lord is greater than prejudice, which is why he was not afraid to address the Samaritan woman: mercy is greater than prejudice. We must learn this well! Mercy is greater than prejudice, and Jesus is so very merciful, very! The outcome of that encounter by the well was the woman's transformation: "the woman left her water jar" (John 4:28), with which she had come to draw water, and ran to the city to tell people about her extraordinary experience. "I found a man who told me all that I ever did. Can this be the Christ?" (verse 29). She was excited. She had gone to draw water from the well, but she found another kind of water, the living water of mercy from which gushes forth eternal life. She found the water she had always sought! She runs to the village, that village which had judged her, condemned her, and rejected her, and she announces that she has met the Messiah: the one who has changed her life. Because every encounter with Jesus changes our lives, always. It is a step forward, a step closer to God. And thus every encounter with Jesus changes our life. It is always, always this way.

In this Gospel passage, we likewise find the impetus to "leave behind our water jar," the symbol of everything that is seemingly important, but loses all its value before the "love of God." We all have one, or more than one! I ask you, and myself: "What is your interior water jar, the one that weighs you down, that distances you from God?" Let us set it aside a little, and with our hearts, let us hear the voice of Jesus offering us another kind of water, another water that brings us close to the Lord. We are called to rediscover the importance and the sense of our Christian life, initiated in Baptism and, like the Samaritan woman, to witness to our brothers. A witness of what? Joy! To witness to the joy of the encounter with Jesus; for, as I said, every encounter with Jesus changes our life, and every encounter with Jesus also fills us with joy, the joy that comes from within. And the Lord is like this. And so we must tell of the marvelous things the Lord can do in our hearts when we have the courage to set aside our own water jar.

—Angelus Address, St. Peter's Square,
Third Sunday of Lent, March 23, 2014

Understand!

1. Jesus sat by the well at the sixth hour, noontime. Normally, women came to draw water earlier, in the cooler part of the day. Why do you think this woman came at noon?

2. Jews did not associate with Samaritans in Jesus' time, yet Jesus initiated a conversation with a Samaritan woman. What was he trying to teach his disciples by his example?

3. Jesus surprised the woman by speaking to her instead of ignoring or rejecting her. She was amazed at all that he knew about her life. What do her actions reveal about how she felt when she encountered Jesus and his mercy?

_____

_____

_____

_____

_____

_____

4. Jesus spoke truthfully and directly to the woman about her life but did not condemn her. How did Jesus communicate his love, which helped her to face her sin and open her heart to Jesus?

_____

_____

_____

_____

_____

5. Jesus tells the disciples, "I have food to eat of which you do not know," and he rejoices in "the harvest" (John 4:32, 35). What does he mean? Why is he rejoicing?

_____

_____

_____

_____

_____

Grow!

1. What underlying prejudices do you hold that might keep you from extending mercy to another person? That person could be an immigrant, a homeless person, a person of another religion—or an atheist. How can you become more aware of those prejudices and overcome them with mercy?

_____

_____

_____

_____

_____

_____

2. Pope Francis tells us that Jesus might have been thirsty, but his real reason for asking for a drink was to awaken the woman's thirst for God. When do you sense your own inner thirst, your need for God? What makes you unaware of your thirst?

_____

_____

_____

_____

_____

_____

3. Jesus' mercy toward the woman helped her to respond differently to Jesus. She spoke to him not as an enemy but as a friend. When has God's mercy transformed your behavior toward a person who is difficult to love?

_____

_____

_____

_____

_____

_____

4. In her joy at encountering Jesus, the woman ran to her town and told everyone to come and see Jesus. Who do you know who is a joyful witness of Jesus? How has their joy affected you?

_____

_____

_____

_____

_____

_____

5. What are your "water jars"? What are those things in your life that are seemingly important but distance you from God or lose their value when compared to the love of God? Pray to recognize them, and ask Jesus for the grace to leave them behind.

_____

_____

_____

_____

_____

_____

Reflect!

1. In Jesus' time, Gentiles were considered "unclean" and Jews had no contact with them. Yet Peter learned that God wanted the Gentiles to be baptized and become part of God's family. Read Acts 10. Reflect on Peter's statement that "God shows no partiality" (10:34). How might this truth require you to readjust your thinking and attitudes?

2. In the following excerpt from his Bull of Indiction, Pope Francis exhorts us to make this Holy Year of Mercy an opportunity to reach out to those on the margins of society by doing the spiritual and corporal works of mercy. What can you and your family do to serve those in need this year?

In this Holy Year, we look forward to the experience of opening our hearts to those living on the outermost fringes of society: fringes which modern society itself creates. How many uncertain and painful situations there are in the world today! How many are the wounds borne by the flesh of those who have no voice because their cry is muffled and drowned out by the indifference of the rich! During this Jubilee, the Church will be called even more to heal these wounds, to assuage them with the oil of consolation, to bind them with mercy and cure them with solidarity and vigilant care. Let us not fall into humiliating indifference or a monotonous routine that prevents us from discovering what is new! Let us ward off destructive cynicism! Let us open our eyes and see the misery of the world, the wounds of our brothers and sisters who are denied their dignity, and let us recognize that we are compelled to heed their cry for help! May we reach out to them and support them so they can feel the warmth of our presence, our friendship, and our fraternity! May their cry become our own, and together may we break down the barriers of indifference that too often reign supreme and mask our hypocrisy and egoism!

It is my burning desire that, during this Jubilee, the Christian people may reflect on the *corporal and spiritual works of mercy*. It will be a way to reawaken our conscience, too often grown dull in the face of poverty. And let us enter more deeply into the heart of the Gospel where the poor have a special experience of God's mercy. Jesus introduces us to these works of mercy in his preaching so that we can know whether or not we are living as his disciples. Let us rediscover these *corporal works of mercy*: to feed the hungry, give drink to the thirsty, clothe the naked, welcome the stranger, heal the sick, visit the imprisoned, and bury the dead. And let us not forget the *spiritual works of mercy*: to counsel the doubtful, instruct the ignorant, admonish sinners, comfort the afflicted, forgive offenses, bear patiently those who do us ill, and pray for the living and the dead. (Bull of Indiction, *The Face of Mercy,* 15)

Act!

What work of mercy could you do for the poor that would "reawaken" your conscience, which may have "grown dull in the face of poverty"? How might this help you grow in mercy and better appreciate the hardships of those with few resources?

Session 7

THE PATIENCE OF MERCY

"This is so beautiful: our God is a patient father, who always waits for us and waits with his heart in hand to welcome us, to forgive us. He always forgives us if we go to him."

—POPE FRANCIS

Matthew 13:24-30, 36-43

24 Another parable he put before them, saying, "The kingdom of heaven may be compared to a man who sowed good seed in his field; 25 but while men were sleeping, his enemy came and sowed weeds among the wheat, and went away. 26 So when the plants came up and bore grain, then the weeds appeared also. 27 And the servants of the householder came and said to him, 'Sir, did you not sow good seed in your field? How then has it weeds?' 28 He said to them, 'An enemy has done this.' The servants said to him, 'Then do you want us to go and gather them?' 29 But he said, 'No; lest in gathering the weeds you root up the wheat along with them. 30 Let both grow together until the harvest; and at harvest time I will tell the reapers, Gather the weeds first and bind them in bundles to be burned, but gather the wheat into my barn.'" . . .

36 Then he left the crowds and went into the house. And his disciples came to him, saying, "Explain to us the parable of the weeds of the field." 37 He answered, "He who sows the good seed is the Son of man; 38 the field is the world, and the good seed means the sons of the kingdom; the weeds are the sons of the evil one, 39 and the enemy who sowed them is the devil; the harvest is the close of the age, and the reapers are angels. 40 Just as the weeds are gathered and burned with fire, so will it be at the close of the age. 41 The Son of man will send his angels, and they will gather out of his kingdom all causes of sin and all evildoers, 42 and throw them into the furnace of fire; there men will weep and gnash their teeth. 43 Then the righteous will shine like the sun in the kingdom of their Father. He who has ears, let him hear."

Words of Pope Francis

These Sundays the liturgy proposes several Gospel *parables*, that is, short stories which Jesus used to announce the kingdom of heaven to the crowds. Among those in today's Gospel, there is a rather complex one which Jesus explained to the disciples: it is that of *the good grain and the weed*, which deals with *the problem of evil* in the world and calls attention to *God's patience* (cf. Matthew 13:24-30, 36-43). The story takes place in a field where the owner sows grain, but during the night his enemy comes and sows weed, a term which in Hebrew derives from the same root as the name "Satan" and which alludes to the concept of division. We all know that the demon is a "sower of weed," one who always seeks to sow division between individuals, families, nations, and peoples. The servants wanted to uproot the weed immediately, but the field owner stopped them, explaining that "in gathering the weeds you root up the wheat along with them" (13:29). Because we all know that a weed, when it grows, looks very much like good grain, and there is the risk of confusing them.

The teaching of the parable is twofold. First of all, it tells that the evil in the world *comes not from God but from his enemy, the evil one*. It is curious that the evil one goes at night to sow weed, in the dark, in confusion; he goes where there is no light to sow weed. This enemy is astute: he sows evil in the middle of good; thus it is impossible for us men to distinctly separate them; but God, in the end, will be able to do so.

And here we arrive at the second theme: the juxtaposition of the impatience of the servants and the *patient waiting* of the field owner, who represents God. At times we are in a great hurry to judge, to categorize, to put the good here, the bad there. . . . But remember the prayer of that self-righteous man: "God, I thank you that I am good, that I am not like other men, malicious" (cf. Luke 18:11-12). God, however, knows how to wait. With patience and mercy he gazes into the "field" of life of every person; he sees much better than we do the filth and the evil, but he also sees the seeds of good and waits with trust for them to grow. God is patient; he knows how to wait. This is so beautiful: our God is a patient father, who always waits for us and waits with his heart in hand to welcome us, to forgive us. He always forgives us if we go to him.

The field owner's attitude is that of hope grounded in the certainty that evil does not have the first nor the last word. And it is thanks to this *patient hope* of God that the same weed, which is the malicious heart with so many sins, in the end can become good grain. But be careful: evangelical patience is not indifference to evil; one must not confuse good and evil! In facing weeds in the world, the Lord's disciple is called to imitate the patience of God, to nourish hope with the support of indestructible trust in the final victory of good, that is, of God.

In the end, in fact, evil will be removed and eliminated: at the time of harvest, that is, of judgment, the harvesters will follow the orders of the field owner, separating the weed to burn it (cf. Matthew 13:30). On the day of the final harvest, *the judge will be Jesus,* he who has sown good grain in the world and who himself became the *"grain of wheat,"* who died and rose. In the end we will all be judged by the same measure with which we have judged: *the mercy we have shown to others will also be shown to us.* Let us ask Our Lady, our Mother, to help us to grow in patience, in hope, and in mercy with all brothers and sisters.

—Angelus Address, St. Peter's Square,
Sixteenth Sunday in Ordinary Time, July 20, 2014

Understand!

1. Jesus tells this parable immediately following the parable of the sower and the seed, where he explains that the seed represents the good news of the kingdom of God and the field, the hearts of believers. In this parable, however, the "enemy" doesn't steal away the seed—he plants weeds. What is Jesus trying to teach his disciples about the work of the evil one?

_____

_____

_____

_____

_____

_____

2. The servants wanted to uproot the weeds immediately, recognizing them among the grain in the field. Why did the field owner stop them? What is his primary concern?

_____

_____

_____

_____

_____

_____

3. What does the patience of the field owner show us about God's merciful character?

_____

_____

_____

_____

_____

_____

4. What does this parable teach us about the problem of evil coexisting with good in our world? What is Jesus saying about the presence of evil in our lives and in the world?

_____

_____

_____

_____

_____

_____

5. Jesus clearly states that there will be a final judgment at the end of the age and that the righteous will be saved and the evil will be cast out and punished. How do you think he wants people to react to this truth?

_____

_____

_____

_____

_____

_____

Grow!

1. Do you recognize "weeds" from the evil one in your own life? What might crowd out the work of God in your life? Suspicion? Fear? Doubt? Confusion?

_____

_____

_____

_____

_____

_____

2. Pope Francis remarks that the enemy works while we are "sleeping," in the darkness. Share one practice that helps you to "stay awake" and "live in the light" so that you are less vulnerable to seeds of doubt or division being planted in your heart.

_____

_____

_____

_____

_____

_____

3. Do you believe, as Pope Francis says, that evil does not have the final or last word? What might cause you to doubt that truth? How can you maintain hope in the final victory that is God's?

_____

_____

_____

_____

_____

_____

4. In Luke 18:9-14, Jesus contrasts the tax collector praying humbly in the Temple with the self-righteous Pharisee. How can being aware of your own state before God help you grow in patience and mercy toward others?

_____

_____

_____

_____

_____

_____

5. God, our merciful Father, sees clearly every weed in every person's life, yet he lovingly waits in hope and patience for us to turn to him. Are there weeds in your own life that you've been unable or unwilling to allow God to address? Are there weeds in others' lives that you need to stop addressing and so leave the judgment to God?

_____

_____

_____

_____

_____

_____

Reflect!

1. God is capable of changing every heart, even the most evil, and longs to do so. Is there a person or situation that you think is beyond the scope of God's mercy and power? Bring this individual or circumstance before the Lord in prayer, asking Jesus to intervene and to fill you with trust in his ability to work.

2. In Psalm 136, the psalmist repeats, "His mercy endures forever." Pope Francis reminds us that we will be under the merciful gaze of God for all eternity. This means that no matter how dire our circumstances, God's mercy is with us and will never end. Read Pope Francis' reflection below and the text from Psalm 136. Write a few stanzas about your own life, recalling God's action during good and bad times.

"For his mercy endures forever." This is the refrain that repeats after each verse in Psalm 136 as it narrates the history of God's revelation. By virtue of mercy, all the events of the Old Testament are replete with profound salvific import. Mercy renders God's history with Israel a history of salvation. To repeat continually "for his mercy endures forever," as the psalm does, seems to break through the dimensions of space and time, inserting everything into the eternal mystery of love. It is as if to say that not only in history, but for all eternity, man will always be under the merciful gaze of the

Father. It is no accident that the people of Israel wanted to include this psalm—the "Great *Hallel*," as it is called—in its most important liturgical feast days.

Before his passion, Jesus prayed with this psalm of mercy. Matthew attests to this in his Gospel when he says that "when they had sung a hymn" (26:30), Jesus and his disciples went out to the Mount of Olives. While he was instituting the Eucharist as an everlasting memorial of himself and his paschal sacrifice, he symbolically placed this supreme act of revelation in the light of his mercy. Within the very same context of mercy, Jesus entered upon his passion and death conscious of the great mystery of love that he would consummate on the cross. Knowing that Jesus himself prayed this psalm makes it even more important for us as Christians, challenging us to take up the refrain in our daily lives by praying these words of praise: "For his mercy endures forever." (Bull of Indiction, *The Face of Mercy*, 7)

Act!

Jesus tells us, " Judge not, and you will not be judged; condemn not, and you will not be condemned; forgive, and you will be forgiven; give, and it will be given to you; good measure, pressed down, shaken together, running over, will be put into your lap. For the measure you give will be the measure you get back" (Luke 6:37-38). Is there someone who has wronged you whom you need to forgive? Pray for the grace of God's merciful patience: to leave the judgment to God and let go of bitterness. Reach out in forgiveness and begin anew.

Session 8

MERCY AND NEW LIFE

"Only the power of Jesus can help us come out of these atrophied zones of the heart, these tombs of sin, which we all have."

—POPE FRANCIS

John 11:1-45

[1]Now a certain man was ill, Lazarus of Bethany, the village of Mary and her sister Martha. [2]It was Mary who anointed the Lord with ointment and wiped his feet with her hair, whose brother Lazarus was ill. [3]So the sisters sent to him, saying, "Lord, he whom you love is ill." [4]But when Jesus heard it he said, "This illness is not unto death; it is for the glory of God, so that the Son of God may be glorified by means of it."

[5]Now Jesus loved Martha and her sister and Lazarus. [6]So when he heard that he was ill, he stayed two days longer in the place where he was. [7]Then after this he said to the disciples, "Let us go into Judea again." [8]The disciples said to him, "Rabbi, the Jews were but now seeking to stone you, and are you going there again?" [9]Jesus answered, "Are there not twelve hours in the day? If any one walks in the day, he does not stumble, because he sees the light of this world. [10]But if any one walks in the night, he stumbles, because the light is not in him." [11]Thus he spoke, and then he said to them, "Our friend Lazarus has fallen asleep, but I go to awake him out of sleep." [12]The disciples said to him, "Lord, if he has fallen asleep, he will recover." [13]Now Jesus had spoken of his death, but they thought that he meant taking rest in sleep. [14]Then Jesus told them plainly, "Lazarus is dead; [15]and for your sake I am glad that I was not there, so that you may believe. But let us go to him." [16]Thomas, called the Twin, said to his fellow disciples, "Let us also go, that we may die with him."

[17]Now when Jesus came, he found that Lazarus had already been in the tomb four days. [18]Bethany was near Jerusalem, about

two miles off, ¹⁹ and many of the Jews had come to Martha and Mary to console them concerning their brother. ²⁰ When Martha heard that Jesus was coming, she went and met him, while Mary sat in the house. ²¹ Martha said to Jesus, "Lord, if you had been here, my brother would not have died. ²² And even now I know that whatever you ask from God, God will give you." ²³ Jesus said to her, "Your brother will rise again." ²⁴ Martha said to him, "I know that he will rise again in the resurrection at the last day." ²⁵ Jesus said to her, "I am the resurrection and the life; he who believes in me, though he die, yet shall he live, ²⁶ and whoever lives and believes in me shall never die. Do you believe this?" ²⁷ She said to him, "Yes, Lord; I believe that you are the Christ, the Son of God, he who is coming into the world."

²⁸ When she had said this, she went and called her sister Mary, saying quietly, "The Teacher is here and is calling for you." ²⁹ And when she heard it, she rose quickly and went to him. ³⁰ Now Jesus had not yet come to the village, but was still in the place where Martha had met him. ³¹ When the Jews who were with her in the house, consoling her, saw Mary rise quickly and go out, they followed her, supposing that she was going to the tomb to weep there. ³² Then Mary, when she came where Jesus was and saw him, fell at his feet, saying to him, "Lord, if you had been here, my brother would not have died." ³³ When Jesus saw her weeping, and the Jews who came with her also weeping, he was deeply moved in spirit and troubled; ³⁴ and he said, "Where have you laid him?" They said to him, "Lord, come and see." ³⁵ Jesus wept. ³⁶ So the Jews said, "See how he loved him!" ³⁷ But some of them said, "Could not he who opened the eyes of the blind man have kept this man from dying?"

³⁸ Then Jesus, deeply moved again, came to the tomb; it was a cave, and a stone lay upon it. ³⁹ Jesus said, "Take away the stone." Martha, the sister of the dead man, said to him, "Lord, by this time there will be an odor, for he has been dead four days." ⁴⁰ Jesus said to her, "Did I not tell you that if you would believe you would see the glory of God?" ⁴¹ So they took away the stone. And Jesus lifted up his eyes and said, "Father, I thank thee that thou hast heard me. ⁴² I knew that thou hearest me always, but I have said this on account of the people standing by, that they may believe that thou didst send me." ⁴³ When he had said this, he cried with a loud voice, "Lazarus, come out." ⁴⁴ The dead man came out, his hands and feet bound with bandages, and his face wrapped with a cloth. Jesus said to them, "Unbind him, and let him go."

⁴⁵ Many of the Jews therefore, who had come with Mary and had seen what he did, believed in him.

Words of Pope Francis

Today's three readings speak to us about the resurrection, they speak to us about life. This beautiful promise from the Lord: "Behold I will open your graves, and raise you from your graves" (Ezekiel 37:12), is the promise of the Lord who possesses life and has the power to give life, that those who are dead might regain life. The second reading tells us that we are under the Holy Spirit and that Christ in us, his Spirit, will raise us. And in the third reading of the Gospel [John 11:1-45], we saw how Jesus gave life to Lazarus. Lazarus, who was dead, has returned to life.

I would simply like to say something very briefly. We all have within us some areas, some parts of our heart that are not alive, that are a little dead; and some of us have many dead places in our hearts, a true spiritual necrosis! And when we are in this situation, we know it, we want to get out, but we can't. Only the power of Jesus, the power of Jesus can help us come out of these atrophied zones of the heart, these tombs of sin, which we all have. We are all sinners! But if we become very attached to these tombs and guard them within us and do not will that our whole heart rise again to life, we become corrupted and our soul begins to give off, as Martha says, an "odor" (John 11:39), the stench of a person who is attached to sin. And Lent is something to do with this. Because all of us, who are sinners, do not end up attached to sin, but that we can hear what Jesus said to Lazarus: "He cried out with a loud voice: 'Lazarus, come out'" (11:43).

Today I invite you to think for a moment, in silence, here: where is my interior necrosis? Where is the dead part of my soul? Where is my tomb? Think, for a short moment, all of you in silence. Let us think: what part of the heart can be corrupted because of my attachment to sin, one sin or another? And to remove the stone, to take away the stone of shame and allow the Lord to say to us, as he said to Lazarus: "Come out!" That all our soul might be healed, might be raised by the love of Jesus, by the power of Jesus. He is capable of forgiving us. We all need it! All of us. We are all sinners, but we must be careful not to become corrupt! Sinners we may be, but he forgives us. Let us hear that voice of Jesus who, by the power of God, says to us: "Come out! Leave that tomb you have within you.

Come out. I give you life, I give you happiness, I bless you, I want you for myself."

May the Lord today, on this Sunday, which speaks so much about the resurrection, give us all the grace to rise from our sins, to come out of our tombs; with the voice of Jesus, calling us to go out, to go to him.

—Homily, Pastoral Visit to the
Roman Parish of *San Gregorio Magno*,
Fifth Sunday of Lent, April 6, 2014

Understand!

1. Jesus had a very close relationship with Lazarus and his sisters. Why do you think Jesus waited two days before going to Bethany to see his sick friend Lazarus?

_____

_____

_____

_____

_____

2. God doesn't will or create sickness, but Jesus says that Lazarus' sickness will be for the glory of God and that he will be glorified in it. How does the raising of Lazarus demonstrate God's mercy in bringing good even out of sickness and suffering?

_____

_____

_____

_____

_____

_____

3. In Luke 10:38-42, Martha seems to be portrayed negatively, missing the importance of sitting at Jesus' feet and listening to him. Here, Martha boldly professes her faith in Jesus as the Son of God with the power to heal. What does her example teach us about responding to difficult situations with faith?

_____

_____

_____

_____

_____

_____

4. Why does John include the detail that "Jesus wept"(11:35) when he saw Mary's grief? Why do you think Jesus wept then, and why does he weep today?

_____

_____

_____

_____

_____

_____

5. What is the significance of Lazarus' bandages? What do you think they symbolize?

_____

_____

_____

_____

_____

Grow!

1. Lazarus had been dead for four days, a seemingly hopeless situation. In which situations in your own life or in the lives of your loved ones do you lack hope? What might help you to combat discouragement and grow in trust of God's power and promises?

_____

_____

_____

_____

_____

_____

2. The disciples discouraged Jesus from going to Judea
   because of their fear of what might happen to Jesus there.
   Do you see fear limiting your ability to walk with confi-
   dence in God's plan? What lies behind your fear? Is it past
   hurts? A sense that a person or even God has abandoned
   you before?

_____

_____

_____

_____

_____

3. Martha had faith that Lazarus would rise again on the
   last day, but Jesus invited her to have faith that God could
   raise him that very day, that Lazarus could have new life
   right then and there. Do you struggle to believe that the
   elements of your faith can be true and tangible, not just in
   the afterlife, but here and now? Why or why not?

_____

_____

_____

4. Where are the "dead places" in your heart? Are you attached to these "tombs," as Pope Francis calls them? How might this lead to corruption? What does the Holy Father recommend doing so that we do not begin to give off an "odor"?

_____

_____

_____

_____

_____

_____

5. At our baptism, we received a new spiritual life just as Lazarus received a new physical life. What can you do this week to keep your spiritual life healthy and growing?

_____

_____

_____

_____

_____

_____

Reflect!

1. Just as Jesus told the Jews to roll away the stone in front of Lazarus' tomb, Jesus promises us through the prophet Ezekiel that he will open our graves. Read Ezekiel 37:12-14 and Romans 8:8-11. Pray to hear the Lord's call of mercy. What are the "stones" in your life that God needs to roll away in order to call you forth to new life? Shame? Fear? Hurt? Unbelief in God's mercy? Ask God to remove those obstacles. Bring the "dead places" in your soul to the Lord in prayer and in Confession, and ask Jesus to set you free.

2. Pope Francis speaks of the Year of Mercy as a time of bringing the good news to the poor and freedom to the captives. How can you make the "the preaching of Jesus visible once more"? Using the Holy Father's suggestions below, pray about what God might be calling you to do to extend God's mercy to others during this Jubilee Year.

> In the Gospel of Luke, we find another important element that will help us live the Jubilee with faith. Luke writes that Jesus, on the Sabbath, went back to Nazareth and, as was his custom, entered the synagogue. They called upon him to read the Scripture and to comment on it. The passage was from the Book of Isaiah where it is written: "The Spirit of the Lord God is upon me, because the Lord has anointed me to bring good tidings to the afflicted; he has sent me to bind up the brokenhearted, to proclaim liberty to the captives, and freedom to those in captivity; to proclaim the year of the

Lord's favor" (Isaiah 61:1-2). A "year of the Lord's favor" or "mercy": this is what the Lord proclaimed and this is what we wish to live now. This Holy Year will bring to the fore the richness of Jesus' mission echoed in the words of the prophet: to bring a word and gesture of consolation to the poor, to proclaim liberty to those bound by new forms of slavery in modern society, to restore sight to those who can see no more because they are caught up in themselves, to restore dignity to all those from whom it has been robbed. The preaching of Jesus is made visible once more in the response of faith which Christians are called to offer by their witness. May the words of the Apostle accompany us: he who does acts of mercy, let him do them with cheerfulness (cf. Romans 12:8). (Bull of Indiction, *The Face of Mercy*, 16)

Act!

Is there someone you know who is burdened by sin or sadness? Read with him or her the story of the raising of Lazarus and share how Jesus has called you out of your own "dead places." Offer to pray with your friend, trusting that Jesus wants to mercifully call that person out of the tomb to live a new life of joy and freedom.

APPENDIX I

BULL OF INDICTION
OF THE EXTRAORDINARY JUBILEE
OF MERCY

Misericordiae Vultus [The Face of Mercy]

Francis
Bishop of Rome
Servant of the Servants Of God
To All Who Read This Letter
Grace, Mercy, and Peace

1. Jesus Christ is the face of the Father's mercy. These words
might well sum up the mystery of the Christian faith. Mercy
has become living and visible in Jesus of Nazareth, reaching
its culmination in him. The Father, "rich in mercy" (*Eph* 2:4),
after having revealed his name to Moses as "a God merciful
and gracious, slow to anger, and abounding in steadfast love
and faithfulness" (*Ex* 34:6), has never ceased to show, in various ways throughout history, his divine nature. In the "fullness of time" (*Gal* 4:4), when everything had been arranged
according to his plan of salvation, he sent his only Son into the
world, born of the Virgin Mary, to reveal his love for us in a
definitive way. Whoever sees Jesus sees the Father (cf. *Jn* 14:9).
Jesus of Nazareth, by his words, his actions, and his entire person,[1] reveals the mercy of God.

2. We need constantly to contemplate the mystery of mercy. It is a wellspring of joy, serenity, and peace. Our salvation depends on it. Mercy: the word reveals the very mystery of the Most Holy Trinity. Mercy: the ultimate and supreme act by which God comes to meet us. Mercy: the fundamental law that dwells in the heart of every person who looks sincerely into the eyes of his brothers and sisters on the path of life. Mercy: the bridge that connects God and man, opening our hearts to the hope of being loved forever despite our sinfulness.

3. At times we are called to gaze even more attentively on mercy so that we may become a more effective sign of the Father's action in our lives. For this reason I have proclaimed an *Extraordinary Jubilee of Mercy* as a special time for the Church, a time when the witness of believers might grow stronger and more effective.

The Holy Year will open on December 8, 2015, the Solemnity of the Immaculate Conception. This liturgical feast day recalls God's action from the very beginning of the history of mankind. After the sin of Adam and Eve, God did not wish to leave humanity alone in the throes of evil. And so he turned his gaze to Mary, holy and immaculate in love (cf. *Eph* 1:4), choosing her to be the Mother of man's Redeemer. When faced with the gravity of sin, God responds with the fullness of mercy. Mercy will always be greater than any sin, and no one can place limits on the love of God who is ever ready to forgive. I will have the joy of opening the Holy Door on the Solemnity of the Immaculate Conception. On that day, the Holy Door will become a *Door of Mercy* through which anyone who enters will experience the love of God who consoles, pardons, and instills hope.

On the following Sunday, the Third Sunday of Advent, the Holy Door of the Cathedral of Rome—that is, the Basilica of Saint John Lateran—will be opened. In the following weeks, the Holy Doors of the other Papal Basilicas will be opened. On the same Sunday, I will announce that in every local church, at the cathedral—the mother church of the faithful in any particular area—or, alternatively, at the co-cathedral or another church of special significance, a Door of Mercy will be opened for the duration of the Holy Year. At the discretion of the local ordinary, a similar door may be opened at any shrine frequented by large groups of pilgrims, since visits to these holy sites are so often grace-filled moments, as people discover a path to conversion. Every Particular Church, therefore, will be directly involved in living out this Holy Year as an extraordinary moment of grace and spiritual renewal. Thus the Jubilee will be celebrated both in Rome and in the Particular Churches as a visible sign of the Church's universal communion.

4. I have chosen the date of December 8 because of its rich meaning in the recent history of the Church. In fact, I will open the Holy Door on the fiftieth anniversary of the closing of the Second Vatican Ecumenical Council. The Church feels a great need to keep this event alive. With the Council, the Church entered a new phase of her history. The Council Fathers strongly perceived, as a true breath of the Holy Spirit, a need to talk about God to men and women of their time in a more accessible way. The walls which for too long had made the Church a kind of fortress were torn down and the time had come to proclaim the Gospel in a new way. It was a new phase of the same evangelization that had existed from

the beginning. It was a fresh undertaking for all Christians to bear witness to their faith with greater enthusiasm and conviction. The Church sensed a responsibility to be a living sign of the Father's love in the world.

We recall the poignant words of Saint John XXIII when, opening the Council, he indicated the path to follow: "Now the Bride of Christ wishes to use the medicine of mercy rather than taking up arms of severity. . . . The Catholic Church, as she holds high the torch of Catholic truth at this Ecumenical Council, wants to show herself a loving mother to all; patient, kind, moved by compassion and goodness toward her separated children."[2] Blessed Paul VI spoke in a similar vein at the closing of the Council: "We prefer to point out how charity has been the principal religious feature of this Council . . . the old story of the Good Samaritan has been the model of the spirituality of the Council . . . a wave of affection and admiration flowed from the Council over the modern world of humanity. Errors were condemned, indeed, because charity demanded this no less than did truth, but for individuals themselves there was only admonition, respect and love. Instead of depressing diagnoses, encouraging remedies; instead of direful predictions, messages of trust issued from the Council to the present-day world. The modern world's values were not only respected but honored, its efforts approved, its aspirations purified and blessed... Another point we must stress is this: all this rich teaching is channeled in one direction, the service of mankind, of every condition, in every weakness and need."[3]

With these sentiments of gratitude for everything the Church has received, and with a sense of responsibility for the task that lies ahead, we shall cross the threshold of the Holy Door fully confident that the strength of the Risen Lord, who constantly supports us on our pilgrim way, will sustain us. May the Holy Spirit, who guides the steps of believers in cooperating with the work of salvation wrought by Christ, lead the way and support the People of God so that they may contemplate the face of mercy.[4]

5. The Jubilee Year will close with the liturgical Solemnity of Christ the King on November 20, 2016. On that day, as we seal the Holy Door, we shall be filled, above all, with a sense of gratitude and thanksgiving to the Most Holy Trinity for having granted us an extraordinary time of grace. We will entrust the life of the Church, all humanity, and the entire cosmos to the Lordship of Christ, asking him to pour out his mercy upon us like the morning dew, so that everyone may work together to build a brighter future. How much I desire that the year to come will be steeped in mercy, so that we can go out to every man and woman, bringing the goodness and tenderness of God! May the balm of mercy reach everyone, both believers and those far away, as a sign that the kingdom of God is already present in our midst!

6. "It is proper to God to exercise mercy, and he manifests his omnipotence particularly in this way."[5] Saint Thomas Aquinas' words show that God's mercy, rather than a sign of weakness, is the mark of his omnipotence. For this reason the liturgy, in one of its most ancient collects, has us pray: "O God, who reveal your power above all in your mercy and forgiveness . . . "[6] Throughout the history of humanity, God will always be the One who is present, close, provident, holy, and merciful.

"Patient and merciful." These words often go together in the Old Testament to describe God's nature. His being merciful is concretely demonstrated in his many actions throughout the history of salvation where his goodness prevails over punishment and destruction. In a special way the Psalms bring to the fore the grandeur of his merciful action: "He forgives all your iniquity, he heals all your diseases, he redeems your life from the pit, he crowns you with steadfast love and mercy" (*Ps* 103:3-4). Another psalm, in an even more explicit way, attests to the concrete signs of his mercy: "He executes justice for the oppressed; he gives food to the hungry. The Lord sets the prisoners free; the Lord opens the eyes of the blind. The Lord lifts up those who are bowed down; the Lord loves the righteous. The Lord watches over the sojourners, he upholds the widow and the fatherless; but the way of the wicked he brings to ruin" (*Ps* 146:7-9). Here are some other expressions of the Psalmist: "He heals the brokenhearted, and binds up their wounds . . . The Lord lifts up the downtrodden, he casts the wicked to the ground" (*Ps* 147:3, 6). In short, the mercy of God is not an abstract idea, but a concrete reality with which he reveals his love as of that of a father or a mother, moved to the very depths out of love for their child. It is hardly an exaggeration to say that this is a "visceral" love. It gushes forth from the depths naturally, full of tenderness and compassion, indulgence, and mercy.

7. "For his mercy endures forever." This is the refrain that repeats after each verse in Psalm 136 as it narrates the history of God's revelation. By virtue of mercy, all the events of the Old Testament are replete with profound salvific import. Mercy renders God's history with Israel a history of salvation. To repeat continually "for his mercy endures forever," as the psalm does, seems to break through the dimensions of space

and time, inserting everything into the eternal mystery of love. It is as if to say that not only in history, but for all eternity man will always be under the merciful gaze of the Father. It is no accident that the people of Israel wanted to include this psalm—the "Great *Hallel*," as it is called—in its most important liturgical feast days.

Before his Passion, Jesus prayed with this psalm of mercy. Matthew attests to this in his Gospel when he says that, "when they had sung a hymn" (26:30), Jesus and his disciples went out to the Mount of Olives. While he was instituting the Eucharist as an everlasting memorial of himself and his paschal sacrifice, he symbolically placed this supreme act of revelation in the light of his mercy. Within the very same context of mercy, Jesus entered upon his passion and death, conscious of the great mystery of love that he would consummate on the Cross. Knowing that Jesus himself prayed this psalm makes it even more important for us as Christians, challenging us to take up the refrain in our daily lives by praying these words of praise: "For his mercy endures forever."

8. With our eyes fixed on Jesus and his merciful gaze, we experience the love of the Most Holy Trinity. The mission Jesus received from the Father was that of revealing the mystery of divine love in its fullness. "God is love" (*1 Jn* 4:8, 16), John affirms for the first and only time in all of Holy Scripture. This love has now been made visible and tangible in Jesus' entire life. His person is nothing but love, a love given gratuitously. The relationships he forms with the people who approach him manifest something entirely unique and unrepeatable. The signs he works, especially in favor of sinners, the poor, the marginalized, the sick, and the suffering, are all meant to

teach mercy. Everything in him speaks of mercy. Nothing in him is devoid of compassion.

Jesus, seeing the crowds of people who followed him, realized that they were tired and exhausted, lost and without a guide, and he felt deep compassion for them (cf. *Mt* 9:36). On the basis of this compassionate love he healed the sick who were presented to him (cf. *Mt* 14:14), and with just a few loaves of bread and fish he satisfied the enormous crowd (cf. *Mt* 15:37). What moved Jesus in all of these situations was nothing other than mercy, with which he read the hearts of those he encountered and responded to their deepest need. When he came upon the widow of Nain taking her son out for burial, he felt great compassion for the immense suffering of this grieving mother, and he gave back her son by raising him from the dead (cf. *Lk* 7:15). After freeing the demoniac in the country of the Gerasenes, Jesus entrusted him with this mission: "Go home to your friends, and tell them how much the Lord has done for you, and how he has had mercy on you" (*Mk* 5:19). The calling of Matthew is also presented within the context of mercy. Passing by the tax collector's booth, Jesus looked intently at Matthew. It was a look full of mercy that forgave the sins of that man, a sinner and a tax collector, whom Jesus chose—against the hesitation of the disciples—to become one of the Twelve. Saint Bede the Venerable, commenting on this Gospel passage, wrote that Jesus looked upon Matthew with merciful love and chose him: *miserando atque eligendo*.[7] This expression impressed me so much that I chose it for my episcopal motto.

9. In the parables devoted to mercy, Jesus reveals the nature of God as that of a Father who never gives up until he has forgiven the wrong and overcome rejection with compassion and

mercy. We know these parables well, three in particular: the lost sheep, the lost coin, and the father with two sons (cf. *Lk* 15:1-32). In these parables, God is always presented as full of joy, especially when he pardons. In them we find the core of the Gospel and of our faith, because mercy is presented as a force that overcomes everything, filling the heart with love and bringing consolation through pardon.

From another parable, we cull an important teaching for our Christian lives. In reply to Peter's question about how many times it is necessary to forgive, Jesus says: "I do not say seven times, but seventy times seven times" (*Mt* 18:22). He then goes on to tell the parable of the "ruthless servant," who, called by his master to return a huge amount, begs him on his knees for mercy. His master cancels his debt. But he then meets a fellow servant who owes him a few cents and who in turn begs on his knees for mercy, but the first servant refuses his request and throws him into jail. When the master hears of the matter, he becomes infuriated and, summoning the first servant back to him, says, "Should not you have had mercy on your fellow servant, as I had mercy on you?" (*Mt* 18:33). Jesus concludes, "So also my heavenly Father will do to every one of you, if you do not forgive your brother from your heart" (*Mt* 18:35).

This parable contains a profound teaching for all of us. Jesus affirms that mercy is not only an action of the Father; it becomes a criterion for ascertaining who his true children are. In short, we are called to show mercy because mercy has first been shown to us. Pardoning offenses becomes the clearest expression of merciful love, and for us Christians it is an imperative from which we cannot excuse ourselves. At times how hard it seems to forgive! And yet pardon is the instrument placed into our fragile hands to attain serenity of heart. To let go of anger, wrath, violence, and revenge are necessary conditions to living joyfully. Let us therefore heed the Apostle's exhortation: "Do not let the sun go down on your anger" (*Eph* 4:26). Above all, let us listen to the words of Jesus, who made mercy an ideal of life and a criterion for the credibility of our faith: "Blessed are the merciful, for they shall obtain mercy" (*Mt* 5:7): the beatitude to which we should particularly aspire in this Holy Year.

As we can see in Sacred Scripture, mercy is a key word that indicates God's action towards us. He does not limit himself merely to affirming his love, but makes it visible and tangible. Love, after all, can never be just an abstraction. By its very nature, it indicates something concrete: intentions, attitudes, and behaviors that are shown in daily living. The mercy of God is his loving concern for each one of us. He feels responsible; that is, he desires our well-being and he wants to see us happy, full of joy, and peaceful. This is the path which the merciful love of Christians must also travel. As the Father loves, so do his children. Just as he is merciful, so we are called to be merciful to each other.

10. Mercy is the very foundation of the Church's life. All of her pastoral activity should be caught up in the tenderness she makes present to believers; nothing in her preaching and in her witness to the world can be lacking in mercy. The Church's very credibility is seen in how she shows merciful and compassionate love. The Church "has an endless desire to show mercy."[8] Perhaps we have long since forgotten how to show and live the way of mercy. The temptation, on the one hand, to focus exclusively on justice made us forget that this is only the first, albeit necessary and indispensable step. But the Church needs to go

beyond and strive for a higher and more important goal. On the other hand, sad to say, we must admit that the practice of mercy is waning in the wider culture. In some cases the word seems to have dropped out of use. However, without a witness to mercy, life becomes fruitless and sterile, as if sequestered in a barren desert. The time has come for the Church to take up the joyful call to mercy once more. It is time to return to the basics and to bear the weaknesses and struggles of our brothers and sisters. Mercy is the force that reawakens us to new life and instills in us the courage to look to the future with hope.

11. Let us not forget the great teaching offered by Saint John Paul II in his second Encyclical, *Dives in Misericordia*, which at the time came unexpectedly, its theme catching many by surprise. There are two passages in particular to which I would like to draw attention. First, Saint John Paul II highlighted the fact that we had forgotten the theme of mercy in today's cultural milieu: "The present-day mentality, more perhaps than that of people in the past, seems opposed to a God of mercy, and in fact tends to exclude from life and to remove from the human heart the very idea of mercy. The word and the concept of 'mercy' seem to cause uneasiness in man, who, thanks to the enormous development of science and technology, never before known in history, has become the master of the earth and has subdued and dominated it (cf. *Gen* 1:28). This dominion over the earth, sometimes understood in a one-sided and superficial way, seems to have no room for mercy. . . . And this is why, in the situation of the Church and the world today, many individuals and groups guided by a lively sense of faith are turning, I would say almost spontaneously, to the mercy of God."[9]

Furthermore, Saint John Paul II pushed for a more urgent proclamation and witness to mercy in the contemporary world: "It is dictated by love for man, for all that is human and which, according to the intuitions of many of our contemporaries, is threatened by an immense danger. The mystery of Christ . . . obliges me to proclaim mercy as God's merciful love, revealed in that same mystery of Christ. It likewise obliges me to have recourse to that mercy and to beg for it at this difficult, critical phase of the history of the Church and of the world."[10] This teaching is more pertinent than ever and deserves to be taken up once again in this Holy Year. Let us listen to his words once more: "The Church lives an authentic life when she professes and proclaims mercy—the most stupendous attribute of the Creator and of the Redeemer—and when she brings people close to the sources of the Savior's mercy, of which she is the trustee and dispenser."[11]

12. The Church is commissioned to announce the mercy of God, the beating heart of the Gospel, which in its own way must penetrate the heart and mind of every person. The Spouse of Christ must pattern her behavior after the Son of God, who went out to everyone without exception. In the present day, as the Church is charged with the task of the new evangelization, the theme of mercy needs to be proposed again and again with new enthusiasm and renewed pastoral action. It is absolutely essential for the Church and for the credibility of her message that she herself live and testify to mercy. Her language and her gestures must transmit mercy, so as to touch the hearts of all people and inspire them once more to find the road that leads to the Father.

The Church's first truth is the love of Christ. The Church makes herself a servant of this love and mediates it to all people: a love that forgives and expresses itself in the gift of oneself. Consequently, wherever the Church is present, the mercy of the Father must be evident. In our parishes, communities, associations, and movements, in a word, wherever there are Christians, everyone should find an oasis of mercy.

13. We want to live this Jubilee Year in light of the Lord's words: *Merciful like the Father.* The Evangelist reminds us of the teaching of Jesus who says, "Be merciful just as your Father is merciful" (*Lk* 6:36). It is a program of life as demanding as it is rich with joy and peace. Jesus's command is directed to anyone willing to listen to his voice (cf. *Lk* 6:27). In order to be capable of mercy, therefore, we must first of all dispose ourselves to listen to the Word of God. This means rediscovering the value of silence in order to meditate on the Word that comes to us. In this way, it will be possible to contemplate God's mercy and adopt it as our lifestyle.

14. The practice of *pilgrimage* has a special place in the Holy Year, because it represents the journey each of us makes in this life. Life itself is a pilgrimage, and the human being is a *viator*, a pilgrim traveling along the road, making his way to the desired destination. Similarly, to reach the Holy Door in Rome or in any other place in the world, everyone, each according to his or her ability, will have to make a pilgrimage. This will be a sign that mercy is also a goal to reach and requires dedication and sacrifice. May pilgrimage be an impetus to conversion: by crossing the threshold of the Holy Door, we will find

the strength to embrace God's mercy and dedicate ourselves to being merciful with others as the Father has been with us.

The Lord Jesus shows us the steps of the pilgrimage to attain our goal: "Judge not, and you will not be judged; condemn not, and you will not be condemned; forgive, and you will be forgiven; give, and it will be given to you; good measure, pressed down, shaken together, running over, will be put into your lap. For the measure you give will be the measure you get back" (*Lk* 6:37-38). The Lord asks us above all *not to judge* and *not to condemn.* If anyone wishes to avoid God's judgment, he should not make himself the judge of his brother or sister. Human beings, whenever they judge, look no farther than the surface, whereas the Father looks into the very depths of the soul. How much harm words do when they are motivated by feelings of jealousy and envy! To speak ill of others puts them in a bad light, undermines their reputation, and leaves them prey to the whims of gossip. To refrain from judgment and condemnation means, in a positive sense, to know how to accept the good in every person and to spare him any suffering that might be caused by our partial judgment, our presumption to know everything about him. But this is still not sufficient to express mercy. Jesus asks us also to *forgive* and to *give.* To be instruments of mercy because it was we who first received mercy from God. To be generous with others, knowing that God showers his goodness upon us with immense generosity.

Merciful like the Father, therefore, is the "motto" of this Holy Year. In mercy, we find proof of how God loves us. He gives his entire self, always, freely, asking nothing in return. He comes to our aid whenever we call upon him. What a beautiful thing that the Church begins her daily prayer with the words, "O God, come to my assistance. O Lord, make haste to help me" (*Ps* 70:2)!

The assistance we ask for is already the first step of God's mercy toward us. He comes to assist us in our weakness. And his help consists in helping us accept his presence and closeness to us. Day after day, touched by his compassion, we also can become compassionate towards others.

15. In this Holy Year, we look forward to the experience of opening our hearts to those living on the outermost fringes of society: fringes which modern society itself creates. How many uncertain and painful situations there are in the world today! How many are the wounds borne by the flesh of those who have no voice because their cry is muffled and drowned out by the indifference of the rich! During this Jubilee, the Church will be called even more to heal these wounds, to assuage them with the oil of consolation, to bind them with mercy and cure them with solidarity and vigilant care. Let us not fall into humiliating indifference or a monotonous routine that prevents us from discovering what is new! Let us ward off destructive cynicism! Let us open our eyes and see the misery of the world, the wounds of our brothers and sisters who are denied their dignity, and let us recognize that we are compelled to heed their cry for help! May we reach out to them and support them so they can feel the warmth of our presence, our friendship, and our fraternity! May their cry become our own, and together may we break down the barriers of indifference that too often reign supreme and mask our hypocrisy and egoism!

It is my burning desire that, during this Jubilee, the Christian people may reflect on the *corporal and spiritual works of mercy*. It will be a way to reawaken our conscience, too often grown dull in the face of poverty. And let us enter more deeply into the heart of the Gospel where the poor have a special experience of God's mercy. Jesus introduces us to these works of mercy in his preaching so that we can know whether or not we are living as his disciples. Let us rediscover these *corporal works of mercy*: to feed the hungry, give drink to the thirsty, clothe the naked, welcome the stranger, heal the sick, visit the imprisoned, and bury the dead. And let us not forget the *spiritual works of mercy:* to counsel the doubtful, instruct the ignorant, admonish sinners, comfort the afflicted, forgive offenses, bear patiently those who do us ill, and pray for the living and the dead.

We cannot escape the Lord's words to us, and they will serve as the criteria upon which we will be judged: whether we have fed the hungry and given drink to the thirsty, welcomed the stranger and clothed the naked, or spent time with the sick and those in prison (cf. *Mt* 25:31-45). Moreover, we will be asked if we have helped others to escape the doubt that causes them to fall into despair and which is often a source of loneliness; if we have helped to overcome the ignorance in which millions of people live, especially children deprived of the necessary means to free them from the bonds of poverty; if we have been close to the lonely and afflicted; if we have forgiven those who have offended us and have rejected all forms of anger and hate that lead to violence; if we have had the kind of patience God shows, who is so patient with us; and if we have commended our brothers and sisters to the Lord in prayer. In each of these "little ones," Christ himself is present. His flesh becomes visible in the flesh of the tortured, the crushed, the scourged, the malnourished, and the exiled . . . to be acknowledged, touched, and cared for by us. Let us not forget the words of Saint John of the Cross: "As we prepare to leave this life, we will be judged on the basis of love."[12]

16. In the Gospel of Luke, we find another important element that will help us live the Jubilee with faith. Luke writes that Jesus, on the Sabbath, went back to Nazareth and, as was his custom, entered the synagogue. They called upon him to read the Scripture and to comment on it. The passage was from the Book of Isaiah where it is written: "The Spirit of the Lord God is upon me, because the Lord has anointed me to bring good tidings to the afflicted; he has sent me to bind up the broken-hearted, to proclaim liberty to the captives, and freedom to those in captivity; to proclaim the year of the Lord's favor" (*Is* 61:1-2). A "year of the Lord's favor" or "mercy": this is what the Lord proclaimed and this is what we wish to live now. This Holy Year will bring to the fore the richness of Jesus' mission echoed in the words of the prophet: to bring a word and gesture of consolation to the poor, to proclaim liberty to those bound by new forms of slavery in modern society, to restore sight to those who can see no more because they are caught up in themselves, to restore dignity to all those from whom it has been robbed. The preaching of Jesus is made visible once more in the response of faith which Christians are called to offer by their witness. May the words of the Apostle accompany us: he who does acts of mercy, let him do them with cheerfulness (cf. *Rom* 12:8).

17. The season of Lent during this Jubilee Year should also be lived more intensely as a privileged moment to celebrate and experience God's mercy. How many pages of Sacred Scripture are appropriate for meditation during the weeks of Lent to help us rediscover the merciful face of the Father! We can repeat the words of the prophet Micah and make them our own: You,

O Lord, are a God who takes away iniquity and pardons sin, who does not hold your anger forever, but are pleased to show mercy. You, Lord, will return to us and have pity on your people. You will trample down our sins and toss them into the depths of the sea (cf. 7:18-19).

The pages of the prophet Isaiah can also be meditated upon concretely during this season of prayer, fasting, and works of charity: "Is not this the fast that I choose: to loosen the bonds of wickedness, to undo the thongs of the yoke, to let the oppressed go free, and to break every yoke? Is it not to share your bread with the hungry, and bring the homeless poor into your house; when you see the naked, to cover him, and not to hide yourself from your own flesh? Then shall your light break forth like the dawn, and your healing shall spring up speedily; your righteousness shall go before you, the glory of the Lord shall be your rear guard. Then you shall call, and the Lord will answer; you shall cry, and he will say, here I am. If you take away from the midst of you the yoke, the pointing of the finger, and speaking wickedness, if you pour yourself out for the hungry and satisfy the desire of the afflicted, then shall your light rise in the darkness and your gloom be as the noonday. And the Lord will guide you continually, and satisfy your desire with good things, and make your bones strong; and you shall be like a watered garden, like a spring of water, whose waters fail not" (58:6-11).

The initiative of *"24 Hours for the Lord,"* to be celebrated on the Friday and Saturday preceding the Fourth Week of Lent, should be implemented in every diocese. So many people, including young people, are returning to the Sacrament of Reconciliation; through this experience they are rediscovering a path back to the Lord, living a moment of intense prayer and finding meaning in their lives. Let us place the Sacrament of Reconciliation at the center once more in such a way that it will enable people to touch the grandeur of God's mercy with their own hands. For every penitent, it will be a source of true interior peace.

I will never tire of insisting that confessors be authentic signs of the Father's mercy. We do not become good confessors automatically. We become good confessors when, above all, we allow ourselves to be penitents in search of his mercy. Let us never forget that to be confessors means to participate in the very mission of Jesus to be a concrete sign of the constancy of divine love that pardons and saves. We priests have received the gift of the Holy Spirit for the forgiveness of sins, and we are responsible for this. None of us wields power over this Sacrament; rather, we are faithful servants of God's mercy through it. Every confessor must accept the faithful as the father in the parable of the prodigal son: a father who runs out to meet his son despite the fact that he has squandered away his inheritance. Confessors are called to embrace the repentant son who comes back home and to express the joy of having him back again. Let us never tire of also going out to the other son who stands outside, incapable of rejoicing, in order to explain to him that his judgment is severe and unjust and meaningless in light of the father's boundless mercy. May confessors not ask useless questions, but like the father in the parable, interrupt the speech prepared ahead of time by the prodigal son, so that confessors will learn to accept the plea for help and mercy pouring from the heart of every penitent. In short, confessors are called to be a sign of the primacy of mercy always, everywhere, and in every situation, no matter what.

18. During Lent of this Holy Year, I intend to send out *Missionaries of Mercy*. They will be a sign of the Church's maternal solicitude for the People of God, enabling them to enter the profound richness of this mystery so fundamental to the faith. There will be priests to whom I will grant the authority to pardon even those sins reserved to the Holy See, so that the breadth of their mandate as confessors will be even clearer. They will be, above all, living signs of the Father's readiness to welcome those in search of his pardon. They will be missionaries of mercy because they will be facilitators of a truly human encounter, a source of liberation, rich with responsibility for overcoming obstacles and taking up the new life of Baptism again. They will be led in their mission by the words of the Apostle: "For God has consigned all men to disobedience, that he may have mercy upon all" (*Rom* 11:32). Everyone, in fact, without exception, is called to embrace the call to mercy. May these Missionaries live this call with the assurance that they can fix their eyes on Jesus, "the merciful and faithful high priest in the service of God" (*Heb* 2:17).

I ask my brother Bishops to invite and welcome these Missionaries so that they can be, above all, persuasive preachers of mercy. May individual dioceses organize "missions to the people" in such a way that these Missionaries may be heralds of joy and forgiveness. Bishops are asked to celebrate the Sacrament of Reconciliation with their people so that the time of grace made possible by the Jubilee Year makes it possible for many of God's sons and daughters to take up once again the journey to the Father's house. May pastors, especially during the liturgical season of Lent, be diligent in calling back the faithful "to the throne of grace, that we may receive mercy and find grace" (*Heb* 4:16).

19. May the message of mercy reach everyone, and may no one be indifferent to the call to experience mercy. I direct this invitation to conversion even more fervently to those whose behavior distances them from the grace of God. I particularly have in mind men and women belonging to criminal organizations of any kind. For their own good, I beg them to change their lives. I ask them this in the name of the Son of God who, though rejecting sin, never rejected the sinner. Do not fall into the terrible trap of thinking that life depends on money and that, in comparison with money, anything else is devoid of value or dignity. This is nothing but an illusion! We cannot take money with us into the life beyond. Money does not bring us happiness. Violence inflicted for the sake of amassing riches soaked in blood makes one neither powerful nor immortal. Everyone, sooner or later, will be subject to God's judgment, from which no one can escape.

The same invitation is extended to those who either perpetrate or participate in corruption. This festering wound is a grave sin that cries out to heaven for vengeance, because it threatens the very foundations of personal and social life. Corruption prevents us from looking to the future with hope, because its tyrannical greed shatters the plans of the weak and tramples upon the poorest of the poor. It is an evil that embeds itself into the actions of everyday life and spreads, causing great public scandal. Corruption is a sinful hardening of the heart that replaces God with the illusion that money is a form of power. It is a work of darkness, fed by suspicion and intrigue. *Corruptio optimi pessima*, Saint Gregory the Great said with good reason, affirming that no one can think himself immune from this temptation. If we want to drive it out from personal and social life, we need prudence, vigilance, loyalty, transparency, together with the courage to denounce any wrongdoing. If it is not combated openly, sooner or later everyone will become an accomplice to it, and it will end up destroying our very existence.

This is the opportune moment to change our lives! This is the time to allow our hearts to be touched! When faced with evil deeds, even in the face of serious crimes, it is the time to listen to the cry of innocent people who are deprived of their property, their dignity, their feelings, and even their very lives. To stick to the way of evil will only leave one deluded and sad. True life is something entirely different. God never tires of reaching out to us. He is always ready to listen, as I am too, along with my brother bishops and priests. All one needs to do is to accept the invitation to conversion and submit oneself to justice during this special time of mercy offered by the Church.

20. It would not be out of place at this point to recall the relationship between *justice* and *mercy*. These are not two contradictory realities, but two dimensions of a single reality that unfolds progressively until it culminates in the fullness of love. Justice is a fundamental concept for civil society, which is meant to be governed by the rule of law. Justice is also understood as that which is rightly due to each individual. In the Bible, there are many references to divine justice and to God as "judge." In these passages, justice is understood as the full observance of the Law and the behavior of every good Israelite in conformity with God's commandments. Such a vision, however, has not infrequently led to legalism by distorting the original meaning of justice and obscuring its profound value. To overcome this legalistic perspective, we need to recall that in Sacred Scripture,

justice is conceived essentially as the faithful abandonment of oneself to God's will.

For his part, Jesus speaks several times of the importance of faith over and above the observance of the law. It is in this sense that we must understand his words when, reclining at table with Matthew and other tax collectors and sinners, he says to the Pharisees raising objections to him, "Go and learn the meaning of 'I desire mercy not sacrifice.' I have come not to call the righteous, but sinners" (*Mt* 9:13). Faced with a vision of justice as the mere observance of the law that judges people simply by dividing them into two groups—the just and sinners—Jesus is bent on revealing the great gift of mercy that searches out sinners and offers them pardon and salvation. One can see why, on the basis of such a liberating vision of mercy as a source of new life, Jesus was rejected by the Pharisees and the other teachers of the law. In an attempt to remain faithful to the law, they merely placed burdens on the shoulders of others and undermined the Father's mercy. The appeal to a faithful observance of the law must not prevent attention from being given to matters that touch upon the dignity of the person.

The appeal Jesus makes to the text from the book of the prophet Hosea—"I desire love and not sacrifice" (6:6)—is important in this regard. Jesus affirms that, from that time onward, the rule of life for his disciples must place mercy at the center, as Jesus himself demonstrated by sharing meals with sinners. Mercy, once again, is revealed as a fundamental aspect of Jesus' mission. This is truly challenging to his hearers, who would draw the line at a formal respect for the law. Jesus, on the other hand, goes beyond the law; the company he keeps with those the law considers sinners makes us realize the depth of his mercy.

The Apostle Paul makes a similar journey. Prior to meeting Jesus on the road to Damascus, he dedicated his life to pursuing the justice of the law with zeal (cf. *Phil* 3:6). His conversion to Christ led him to turn that vision upside down, to the point that he would write to the Galatians: "We have believed in Christ Jesus, in order to be justified by faith in Christ, and not by works of the law, because by works of the law shall no one be justified" (2:16).

Paul's understanding of justice changes radically. He now places faith first, not justice. Salvation comes not through the observance of the law, but through faith in Jesus Christ, who in his death and resurrection brings salvation together with a mercy that justifies. God's justice now becomes the liberating force for those oppressed by slavery to sin and its consequences. God's justice is his mercy (cf. *Ps* 51:11-16).

21. Mercy is not opposed to justice but rather expresses God's way of reaching out to the sinner, offering him a new chance to look at himself, convert, and believe. The experience of the prophet Hosea can help us see the way in which mercy surpasses justice. The era in which the prophet lived was one of the most dramatic in the history of the Jewish people. The kingdom was tottering on the edge of destruction; the people had not remained faithful to the covenant; they had wandered from God and lost the faith of their forefathers. According to human logic, it seems reasonable for God to think of rejecting an unfaithful people; they had not observed their pact with God and therefore deserved just punishment: in other words, exile. The prophet's words attest to this: "They shall not return to the land of Egypt, and Assyria shall be their king, because they have refused to return to me" (*Hos* 11:5). And yet, after

this invocation of justice, the prophet radically changes his speech and reveals the true face of God: "How can I give you up, O Ephraim! How can I hand you over, O Israel! How can I make you like Admah! How can I treat you like Zeboiim! My heart recoils within me, my compassion grows warm and tender. I will not execute my fierce anger, I will not again destroy Ephraim; for I am God and not man, the Holy One in your midst, and I will not come to destroy" (11:8-9). Saint Augustine, almost as if he were commenting on these words of the prophet, says: "It is easier for God to hold back anger than mercy."[13] And so it is. God's anger lasts but a moment, his mercy forever.

If God limited himself to only justice, he would cease to be God, and would instead be like human beings who ask merely that the law be respected. But mere justice is not enough. Experience shows that an appeal to justice alone will result in its destruction. This is why God goes beyond justice with his mercy and forgiveness. Yet this does not mean that justice should be devalued or rendered superfluous. On the contrary: anyone who makes a mistake must pay the price. However, this is just the beginning of conversion, not its end, because one begins to feel the tenderness and mercy of God. God does not deny justice. He rather envelopes it and surpasses it with an even greater event in which we experience love as the foundation of true justice. We must pay close attention to what Saint Paul says if we want to avoid making the same mistake for which he reproaches the Jews of his time: "For, being ignorant of the righteousness that comes from God, and seeking to establish their own, they did not submit to God's righteousness. For Christ is the end of the law, that every one who has faith may be justified" (*Rom* 10:3-4). God's justice is his mercy given to everyone as a grace that flows from the death and resurrection of Jesus Christ. Thus the Cross of Christ is God's judgment on all of us and on the whole world, because through it he offers us the certitude of love and new life.

22. A Jubilee also entails the granting of *indulgences*. This practice will acquire an even more important meaning in the Holy Year of Mercy. God's forgiveness knows no bounds. In the death and resurrection of Jesus Christ, God makes even more evident his love and its power to destroy all human sin. Reconciliation with God is made possible through the paschal mystery and the mediation of the Church. Thus God is always ready to forgive, and he never tires of forgiving in ways that are continually new and surprising. Nevertheless, all of us know well the experience of sin. We know that we are called to perfection (cf. *Mt* 5:48), yet we feel the heavy burden of sin. Though we feel the transforming power of grace, we also feel the effects of sin typical of our fallen state. Despite being forgiven, the conflicting consequences of our sins remain. In the Sacrament of Reconciliation, God forgives our sins, which he truly blots out; and yet sin leaves a negative effect on the way we think and act. But the mercy of God is stronger even than this. It becomes *indulgence* on the part of the Father who, through the Bride of Christ, his Church, reaches the pardoned sinner and frees him from every residue left by the consequences of sin, enabling him to act with charity, to grow in love rather than to fall back into sin.

The Church lives within the communion of the saints. In the Eucharist, this communion, which is a gift from God, becomes a spiritual union binding us to the saints and blessed ones whose number is beyond counting (cf. *Rev* 7:4). Their holiness comes to the aid of our weakness in a way that enables the Church, with her maternal prayers and her way of life, to fortify the weakness of some with the strength of others. Hence, to live the indulgence of the Holy Year means to approach the Father's mercy with the certainty that his forgiveness extends to the entire life of the believer. To gain an indulgence is to experience the holiness of the Church, who bestows upon all the fruits of Christ's redemption, so that God's love and forgiveness may extend everywhere. Let us live this Jubilee intensely, begging the Father to forgive our sins and to bathe us in his merciful "indulgence."

23. There is an aspect of mercy that goes beyond the confines of the Church. It relates us to Judaism and Islam, both of which consider mercy to be one of God's most important attributes. Israel was the first to receive this revelation which continues in history as the source of an inexhaustible richness meant to be shared with all mankind. As we have seen, the pages of the Old Testament are steeped in mercy, because they narrate the works that the Lord performed in favor of his people at the most trying moments of their history. Among the privileged names that Islam attributes to the Creator are "Merciful and Kind." This invocation is often on the lips of faithful Muslims who feel themselves accompanied and sustained by mercy in their daily weakness. They too believe that no one can place a limit on divine mercy because its doors are always open.

I trust that this Jubilee Year celebrating the mercy of God will foster an encounter with these religions and with other noble religious traditions; may it open us to even more fervent dialogue so that we might know and understand one another better; may it eliminate every form of closed-mindedness and disrespect, and drive out every form of violence and discrimination.

24. My thoughts now turn to the Mother of Mercy. May the sweetness of her countenance watch over us in this Holy Year, so that all of us may rediscover the joy of God's tenderness. No one has penetrated the profound mystery of the incarnation like Mary. Her entire life was patterned after the presence of mercy made flesh. The Mother of the Crucified and Risen One has entered the sanctuary of divine mercy because she participated intimately in the mystery of his love.

Chosen to be the Mother of the Son of God, Mary, from the outset, was prepared by the love of God to be the *Ark of the Covenant* between God and man. She treasured divine mercy in her heart in perfect harmony with her Son Jesus. Her hymn of praise, sung at the threshold of the home of Elizabeth, was dedicated to the mercy of God which extends from "generation to generation" (*Lk* 1:50). We too were included in those prophetic words of the Virgin Mary. This will be a source of comfort and strength to us as we cross the threshold of the Holy Year to experience the fruits of divine mercy.

At the foot of the Cross, Mary, together with John, the disciple of love, witnessed the words of forgiveness spoken by Jesus. This supreme expression of mercy towards those who crucified him shows us the point to which the mercy of God can reach. Mary attests that the mercy of the Son of God knows no bounds and extends to everyone, without exception. Let us address her in the words of the *Salve Regina*, a prayer ever ancient and ever new, so that she may never tire of turning her merciful eyes upon us, and make us worthy to contemplate the face of mercy, her Son Jesus.

Our prayer also extends to the saints and blessed ones who made divine mercy their mission in life. I think especially of the great apostle of mercy, Saint Faustina Kowalska. May she, who was called to enter the depths of divine mercy, intercede for us and obtain for us the grace of living and walking always according to the mercy of God and with an unwavering trust in his love.

25. I present, therefore, this Extraordinary Jubilee Year dedicated to living out in our daily lives the mercy which the Father constantly extends to all of us. In this Jubilee Year, let us allow God to surprise us. He never tires of casting open the doors of his heart and of repeating that he loves us and wants to share his love with us. The Church feels the urgent need to proclaim God's mercy. Her life is authentic and credible only when she becomes a convincing herald of mercy. She knows that her primary task, especially at a moment full of great hopes and signs of contradiction, is to introduce everyone to the great mystery of God's mercy by contemplating the face of Christ. The Church is called above all to be a credible witness to mercy, professing it and living it as the core of the revelation of Jesus Christ. From the heart of the Trinity, from the depths of the mystery of God, the great river of mercy wells up and overflows unceasingly. It is a spring that will never run dry, no matter how many people draw from it. Every time someone is in need, he or she can approach it, because the mercy of God never ends. The profundity of the mystery surrounding it is as inexhaustible as the richness which springs up from it.

In this Jubilee Year, may the Church echo the word of God that resounds strong and clear as a message and a sign of pardon, strength, aid, and love. May she never tire of extending mercy, and be ever patient in offering compassion and comfort. May the Church become the voice of every man and woman, and repeat confidently without end: "Be mindful of your mercy, O Lord, and your steadfast love, for they have been from of old" (*Ps* 25:6).

Given in Rome, at Saint Peter's, on April 11, the Vigil of the Second Sunday of Easter, or the Sunday of Divine Mercy, in the year of our Lord 2015, the third of my Pontificate.

FRANCISCUS

1. Cf. Second Vatican Ecumenical Council, Dogmatic Constitution on Divine Revelation (*Dei Verbum*), 4.
2. Opening Address of the Second Vatican Ecumenical Council, (*Gaudet Mater Ecclesia*), 11 October 1962, 2–3.
3. Speech at the Final Public Session of the Second Vatican Ecumenical Council, 7 December 1965.
4. Cf. Second Vatican Ecumenical Council, Dogmatic Constitution on the Church (*Lumen Gentium*), 16; Pastoral Constitution on the Church in the Modern World (*Gaudium et Spes*), 15.
5. Saint Thomas Aquinas, *Summa Theologiae*, II-II, q. 30. a. 4.
6. XXVI Sunday in Ordinary Time. This Collect already appears in the eighth century among the euchological texts of the Gelasian Sacramentary (1198).
7. Cf. *Homily* 22: CCL, 122, 149–151.
8. Apostolic Exhortation *Evangelii Gaudium*, 24.
9. No. 2.
10. Saint John Paul II, Encyclical Letter *Dives in Misericordia*, 15.
11. Ibid., 13.
12. *Words of Light and Love*, 57.
13. *Homilies on the Psalms*, 76, 11.

APPENDIX 2

THE LOGO AND MOTTO FOR THE JUBILEE YEAR

The *logo* and the *motto* together provide a fitting summary of what the Jubilee Year is all about. The motto *Merciful like the Father* (taken from the Gospel of Luke, 6:36) serves as an invitation to follow the merciful example of the Father, who asks us not to judge or condemn but to forgive and to give love and forgiveness without measure (cf. 6:37-38). The logo—the work of Jesuit Father Marko I. Rupnik—presents a small *summa theologiae* of the theme of mercy. In fact, it represents an image quite important to the early Church: that of the Son having taken upon his shoulders the lost soul, demonstrating that it is the love of Christ that brings to completion the mystery of his incarnation culminating in redemption. The logo has been designed in such a way so as to express the profound way in which the Good Shepherd touches the flesh of humanity and does so with a love with the power to change one's life. One particular feature worthy of note is that while the Good Shepherd, in his great mercy, takes humanity upon himself, his eyes are merged with those of man. Christ sees with the eyes of Adam, and Adam, with the eyes of Christ. Every person discovers in Christ the new Adam, one's own humanity and the future that lies ahead, contemplating, in his gaze, the love of the Father.

The scene is captured within the so-called *mandorla* (the shape of an almond), a figure quite important in early and medieval iconography, for it calls to mind the two natures of Christ, divine and human. The three concentric ovals, with colors progressively lighter as we move outward, suggest the movement of Christ, who carries humanity out of the night of sin and death. Conversely, the depth of the darker color suggests the impenetrability of the love of the Father who forgives all.

APPENDIX 3

PRACTICAL POINTERS FOR FAITH-SHARING GROUPS

A faith-sharing or Bible study discussion group—whether through a parish, a prayer group, or a neighborhood—offers us the opportunity to grow not only in our love for God's word, but also in our love for one another. Such groups provide environments in which we can worship and pray together and strengthen our relationships with other Christians. The following guidelines can help a group get started and run smoothly.

Getting Started

- Decide on a regular time and place to meet. Meeting on a regular basis allows the group to maintain continuity without losing momentum from the previous discussion.

- Set a time limit for each session. An hour and a half is a reasonable length of time in which to have a rewarding discussion on the material contained in each of the sessions in this guide. However, the group may find that a longer time is even more advantageous. If it is necessary to limit the meeting to an hour, select sections of the material that are of greatest interest to the group.

- Designate a moderator or facilitator to lead the discussions and keep the meetings on schedule. This person's role is to help preserve good group dynamics by keeping the discussion on track. He or she should help ensure that no one monopolizes the session and that each person—including the shyest or quietest individual—is offered an opportunity to speak. The group may want to ask members to take turns moderating the sessions.

- Provide enough copies of the study guide for each member of the group, and ask everyone to bring a Bible to the meetings. Each session's Scripture text and is printed in full in the guides, but you will find that a Bible is helpful for looking up other passages and cross-references. The translation provided in this guide is the Catholic Edition of the Revised Standard Version. You may also want to refer to other translations to gain additional insights into the text.

- Try to stay faithful to your commitment and attend as many sessions as possible. Not only does regular participation provide coherence and consistency to the group discussions, but it also demonstrates that members value one another and are committed to sharing their lives with one another.

Session Dynamics

- Read the material for each session in advance, and take time to consider the questions and your answers to them. The single most important key to any successful Bible study is having everyone prepared to participate.

- As a courtesy to all members of your group, try to begin and end each session on schedule. Being prompt respects the other commitments of the members and allows enough time for discussion. If the group still has more to discuss at the end of the allotted time, consider continuing the discussion at the next meeting.

- Open the sessions with prayer. A different person could have the responsibility of leading the opening prayer at each session. The prayer could be a spontaneous one, a traditional prayer such as the Our Father, or one that relates to the topic of that particular meeting. The members of the group might also want to begin some of the meetings with a song or hymn. Whatever you choose, ask the Holy Spirit to guide your discussion and study of the Scripture text presented in that session.

- Contribute actively to the discussion. Let the members of the group get to know you, but try to stick to the topic so that you won't divert the discussion from its purpose. And resist the temptation to monopolize the conversation so that everyone will have an opportunity to learn from one another.

- Listen attentively to everyone in the group. Show respect for the other members and their contributions. Encourage, support, and affirm them as they share. Remember that many questions have more than one answer and that the experience of everyone in the group can be enriched by considering a variety of viewpoints.

- If you disagree with someone's observation or answer to a question, do so gently and respectfully, in a way that shows that you value the person who made the comment, and then explain your own point of view. For example, rather than saying, "You're wrong!" or "That's ridiculous!" try something like "I think I see what you're getting at, but I think that Jesus was saying something different in this passage." Be careful to avoid sounding aggressive or argumentative. Then, watch to see how the subsequent discussion unfolds. Who knows? You may come away with a new and deeper perspective.

- Don't be afraid of pauses and reflective moments of silence during the session. People may need some time to think about a question before putting their thoughts into words.

- Maintain and respect confidentiality within the group. Safeguard the privacy and dignity of each member by not repeating what has been shared during the discussion session unless you have been given permission to do so. That way everyone will get the greatest benefit out of the group by feeling comfortable enough to share on a deep, personal level.

- End the session with prayer. Thank God for what you have learned through the discussion, and ask him to help you integrate it into your life.

The Lord blesses all our efforts to come closer to him. As you spend time preparing for and meeting with your small group, be confident in the knowledge that Christ will fill you with wisdom, insight, and grace and the ability to see him at work in your daily life.